DEAL OR NO DEAL

THE OFFICIAL BEHIND THE SCENES GUIDE

DEAL OR NO DEAL

THE OFFICIAL BEHIND THE SCENES GUIDE

WITH

NOEL EDMONDS

endemol u.k.

Written by:

Noel Edmonds, Charlotte Edmonds, Jane Phillimore, Richard Hague, Glenn Hugill

Endemol would like to thank:
John Miles, The Banker, Jane Atkinson, Robbie Williams, Jim Connolly, Ali Lidbetter, Mitch Silcock, Phil Noall, John Davis, Hana Canter, Mathew Clayton, Drew Gardner, Sian Piddington, Seema Khan, and all the Deal or No Deal team.

Additional photography by: Drew Gardner

First published in Great Britain in 2006

1 3 5 7 9 10 8 6 4 2

Text © Endemol UK, 2006

First published in 2006 by Ebury,
an imprint of Ebury Publishing, Random House,
20 Vauxhall Bridge Road, London SW1V 2SA

The Random House Group Limited Reg. No. 954009

Papers used by Ebury are natural, recyclable products made from wood grown in sustainable forests.

Produced for Endemol UK by Essential Works
www.essentialworks.co.uk

Design for Essential Works: Barbara Doherty
Editor for Essential Works: Jane Phillimore

Chapter 2 illustrations: Mitch Silcock

Printed and bound in Germany by Appl

A CIP catalogue record for this book is available from the British Library

ISBN   009192006X

(ISBN   9780091920067 from January 2007)

www.dealornodeal.com

CONTENTS

When the producers of Deal or No Deal first thought about putting on a British version of the show that had been a hit around the world, they had just one name on their very short shortlist of possible presenters. Unfortunately, the shortlist had been handwritten which, as it turned out, was a massive stroke of luck. For instead of calling Neil Edwards, the hired underling given the job of contacting the shortlisted name on his oversized black telephone rang the legendary Noel Edmonds instead...

WELCOME TO DEAL OR NO DEAL

Introduction by Noel Edmonds

I didn't want to present Deal or No Deal. Maybe it was because I'd seen the French version and my French isn't that good, but I watched it and was totally baffled. I remember thinking that I really couldn't see myself hosting such a frenetic and frankly barmy production.

Deal or No Deal? No Deal, thanks…

That's what I originally said to my close friend and agent, John Miles, who'd sent me the tape. He'd been oddly insistent I watch this new show and was suggesting a return to television fronting the British version. When I said 'No', he was gobsmacked at first, but soon launched the most astonishing charm offensive to make me think again. John is an absolutely brilliant operator, and instead of harping on about Deal, he threw me by asking if I would do him the favour of travelling to Leeds to take part in the Countdown auditions to find a replacement for Richard Whiteley. His thinking was that if he got me into a studio, the old spark might be re-ignited into a roaring flame. I think John knows me better than I do.

While Countdown was not for me, John and a few others seemed to think that Deal or No Deal was. Heavy phone calls came from Peter Bazalgette, Chief Executive of Endemol, and Kevin Lygo, Director of Television for Channel 4 and Adam MacDonald, Commissioning Editor of Channel 4 Daytime, insisting (and persisting) in telling me I should get back on the box as the presenter of Deal or No

Deal. After a few weeks, I cracked under the velvet arm-twisting and arrived in Shepherds Bush, London, on a particularly wet and grey summer day to meet the Endemol team. Executive producer Richard Hague and series producer Glenn Hugill were positive and upbeat, and made me feel very much at home.

During rehearsals, it quickly became clear that I have an absolute inability to sit still

Noel Edmonds

The appeal of the game quickly became clear. By role-playing with Dick de Rijk, the Dutch creator of the format, I soon realised the potential to build tension, joke around with the players and generate drama with The Banker. The problem I'd had with the French format was making the game interesting once the players had dealt. However, as soon as you play the game you realise at once that it's incredibly important to find out if the player has made 'the right deal at the right time', or lost hundreds of thousands on the way.

I still have sleepless nights thinking 'what if' I'd turned down Deal or No Deal. You see, I feel totally comfortable with the show, and genuinely believe that

it plays to my strengths and (thankfully) conceals my weaknesses. So here I'd like to say 'thank you' to all those very nice TV executives who put in that little bit of extra effort and persuaded me to get back in the studio (or shed, in this case).

Once I'd agreed to present the show, things moved very fast indeed. It was the beginning of October, and we had to be on air by the end of the month. Before rehearsals, Dick de Rijk – who has a roaring sense of humour – spent a few days explaining the many ways in which the game can unfold. For the UK version, all the complexities of the foreign versions were stripped out. We rejected joke prizes, selection

questions, and half-naked dancing girls (which, to be honest, I am still a little bit disappointed about!).

Early rehearsals were conducted at the Ministry of Sound in London, using members of the public as our contestants. During these rehearsals, it quickly became clear I have an absolute inability to sit still. Originally we had two stools around the central table, one for the player, one for me, but I wasn't comfortable perched on mine. I felt I needed to prowl around to build tension, and so the second stool was soon firewood. Another casualty from the original setup was the autocue. Deal or No Deal is not a scripted show – improvisation is an integral part of the game. The situation changes too quickly and players reactions can never be anticipated and that suits me fine. I like to think on my feet and this new freedom was almost intoxicating.

Deal or No Deal has been such a runaway success from the start that it's difficult to remember just how nervous we all were when the first shows went on air. When the viewing figures started coming in, everyone was absolutely ecstatic. Well, no: to be precise, we were stunned. We have a very young team working on the show in Bristol and they were rightfully jubilant at our almost instant success. I contained my excitement: having been around that bit longer, I know initial audience figures can be dangerously

flattering because of a large number of 'curiosity viewers' who quickly drift away. TV bosses in London sent me a wonderful bottle of vintage champagne, but it remained firmly locked away until we had at least three weeks' broadcasts under our belts. Only then was I prepared to pop the cork and admit that we did indeed seem to have a hit on our hands. Happily, many more bottles of champagne were opened in the following weeks as the ratings went over three million – almost unheard-of for afternoon telly.

TV critic AA Gill, not normally

And to think I nearly turned it down!

Noel Edmonds

a fan of mine or of afternoon TV in general, was first to spot the addictive nature of the show. He was soon backed up by a university professor who claimed that it took just three viewings for the average human being to become hopelessly hooked on Deal or No Deal. To people who say to me that they just don't get what's going on, I tell them that it's simply a show based on the random opening of boxes. It's no secret that the show's success lies in the psychological aspect of the game, watching the most unlikely-seeming player emerge as a dare-devil risk-taker or seeing the shift of power from Banker to player with a long run of blue boxes. The 'Walk of Wealth' is probably the longest stroll in television; it's certainly the most engrossing. I named the stool the 'Crazy Chair' because I have seen so many players change their personality almost completely once they are perched on it.

A Day in the Life of Deal or No Deal

As you'd expect, our working schedule is very hectic and physically demanding. During the first season, I stayed in a hotel about a 30-minute drive from the studio. We filmed three shows a day for two weeks and then had a week off. I was lucky enough to become a resident in a fabulous luxury hotel, where the staff took to calling me 'Major' in recognition of that nutty chap in Fawlty Towers. I deliberately don't stay in the same hotel as the contestants – I shouldn't be around when they let their hair down when filming is over for the day!

My dressing room is now a Winnebago motorhome parked next door to the studio, but when we began it was a meeting room next to the kitchens, which was less than ideal. In fact, it was so unlike a conventional TV dressing room that when Kevin Lygo of Channel 4 visited the set, the crew set me up in a fake dressing room in the toilet. We were hoping Kevin would arrive and be so aghast at the quality of the dressing rooms that he'd immediately sanction plush new ones for us all. But the joke completely backfired, as he simply walked in, said 'Hi' to the make-up girl who was almost bent double under the towel dispenser, and promptly sat on the loo while he told me how wonderful the show was. I still don't know whether he called our bluff or was actually very proud of the Endemol team for keeping a tight rein on the expenditure!

Before filming begins, I like to prepare by reading the daily news sheet which explains how things are going for each of the players in terms of their filming experiences and time off. Each time, the crew and I know which player will take the 'Walk of Wealth', but the players themselves have no idea who it will be. This can create a challenging wardrobe dilemma if the contestant for that day is wearing something that will clash with one of my apparently legendary bright/loud (delete as applicable) shirts. It's helpful for me to study the background of each player and find out their goal for Deal or No Deal. The more I know about them, the more interesting the show becomes, since the quirky facts and characteristics about them bring the show to life. My role is to put the players at ease and ensure that they have the best game possible. I am very much on their side in that all-important battle with The Banker.

I am also acutely aware of how frightening the first TV experience can be, so when a new contestant is brought in, I always introduce myself to them off-camera before filming begins. 'Newbies', as they're affectionately called, are usually absolutely petrified, so I rarely ask them to pass opinion or actively participate in their first few shows. It's important they settle at their own pace and feel comfortable in front of the cameras before being brought into the action.

The mix of players selected for each game is very carefully considered, since the 'chemistry' that builds between them is vital for the success of the show. The players spend a huge amount of time with each other during and between filming, and often establish great friendships. This makes for an amazingly positive atmosphere. There's no competition between them: just because someone wins a large sum of money in one show, it doesn't mean it won't happen again in the next. In fact, it often works there's a run of good luck for the players, perhaps

I've been a big fan of Deal or No Deal since day one. I love the compelling, jeopardy-driven drama of the show, and the nail-biting climax as contestants gamble to win or lose it all. The Banker – the off-stage voice that intimidates the players – is a master-stroke. Having worked with Noel Edmonds in the past, I can put my hand on my heart and say that he is truly brilliant at what he does.
John Stapleton, co-presenter of GMTV's News Hour

materialising from the positive energy produced when someone does well (much to The Banker's disgust, of course).

During filming, I always tell the players to 'play the money, not the game'. But there have been a number of memorable occasions when the player has become so seduced by the atmosphere that all common sense goes out the window. Not that it necessarily ruins everything for them! I am always delighted when a player says the experience of being on the show was enjoyment enough, regardless of the financial reward. And I hope it's true,

because I feel sorry for the contestants who end up with very small sums of money. The thought that they've had a potentially life-changing experience makes it a bit easier to accept.

When the game is over, I have a photo taken with every player and always tell them to enjoy the money before saying goodbye. Wonderfully, I can't think of one contestant who hasn't sent me a card as a thank-you after they've appeared on the show. It is totally unnecessary, of course, but I find it very moving to see how much pleasure this brilliant show can give to so many people.

Dealing With The Notorious Mr Big – The Banker

There are two important things to note about my relationship with The Banker, and our role in the game:

1 I have to ensure that neither I nor The Banker dominate the player.
2 I have to help the player establish a positive relationship with The Banker, and try subtly to guide them away from danger.

Although I'm always on the side of the player, I grudgingly have to concede that in most instances The Banker is fair. I respect the fact that he has to do his job to the very best of his ability. That said, on a number of occasions I think he has been downright nasty – though thankfully, these occasions are

rare. I particularly like it when he can't 'read' the player. He tries to pick up on the tiniest hints the player gives and makes his offers accordingly, and so it's fascinating when a player gets the better of him and leads him spectacularly astray.

Some people have 'played' The Banker brilliantly. One of the most memorable was Jennifer, and not just because she was the biggest winner in season one. Everyone agreed that she brought a strangely positive feeling with her into the studio. There was a genuine buzz around her game. During the commercial break, Jennifer confided she had money worries and told me the amount she was hoping to win to get her out of financial trouble. She had the most incredible game, and was soon rewarded with an offer from The Banker of £52,000. As the only person who also knew it busted the target she'd set herself, you can imagine my utter shock when she said 'No Deal'. Jennifer continued, telling me that she was feeling very lucky and confident that day. She went on to win £120,000. That was some luck and some self-belief!

At the other end of the scale, Sally, a very pretty girl who'd won the heart of every male in the team (including The Banker), had an absolutely disastrous game. She'd once rowed across the Atlantic with her mother, and was one very determined woman. Sally chose to select her boxes based on negative events that had happened during her trans-Atlantic adventure. For example, she chose the number of a boat that had capsized, and an Irish boat that had sunk when the back fell off. Unfortunately, she ended up in the 1p Club. But she's turned her loss into a win, and now earns good money as a motivational trainer, using her experience on Deal or No Deal as part of her programme.

What's amazed us all is the amount of analysis that surrounds every show. In a game where there is no visual extravagance, I suppose the simplest things catch people's attention. My wardrobe especially comes under very close scrutiny – I once received a letter from a little boy asking why I haven't yet used my jet packs. Bless! He was referring to the microphone transmitters that I have to wear on my belt. (I hate to disappoint him though, so perhaps some day I shall rise majestically and fly from the studio at the end of show.)

The fact that you don't see The Banker and instead see my hand reaching for the phone got me thinking one day about making something of it. After dismissing the idea of selling the 'space' for advertising (though that idea took a while to dismiss, in truth), I decided it would be fun to have a code written on my hand, and challenge the viewers to try and crack it. It wasn't long before the newspapers noticed and tried to intepret the signs on my hand. It created some good dramatic moments – in fact Jonathan Ross even accused me of having tattoos!

Most game shows boil down to the binary excitement of winning or losing; Deal or No Deal has an internal tempo that builds and twists like a Hitchcock plot. I've had to forbid myself watching any more.
A.A. Gill, *Sunday Times*

original DOND box as featured in series one and two

Setbacks on set

Deal or No Deal is filmed in the Endemol West studio, situated just off the Bath Road in Bristol. To the untutored eye, it looks like a series of sheds. That's because it is a series of sheds, albeit 'listed' ones – a fact that has caused us some problems during filming. Specifically, the air conditioning isn't brilliant, and the environment has, on occasion, been very trying. During a hot spell in May 2006 the studio got so warm that a member of the audience fainted, and the executive producer had to call off recording for the rest of the day.

One of the most difficult situations was caused by the non-arrival of the studio audience one morning. What on earth was going on? Where were our guests? It turned out there were accidents and road blocks on the main routes into Bristol that day, causing massive traffic jams and preventing people from getting to the studios. Only a handful had battled in, and we were left in a quandary. Various people were sent out to forage for a new audience: the girl next door in Majestic Wines was convinced to join us, and the guys who were fixing our air conditioning downed tools and took a seat. Everyone in the near vicinity rallied round to watch the recording and saved the day.

My four daughters and friends love coming up to Bristol to watch the filming, and everyone at Endemol looks after them incredibly well. The youngest is not allowed to sit in the audience because she's under 18, but the team let her into the gallery where, complete with headset and microphone, she's encouraged to 'produce' the show, ably assisted by a helping of pizza. And she is not the youngest fan of the programme by far. People of all ages love Deal or No Deal. Although many of our viewers are over 50, we also have a massive student following and have been blamed for falling ratings in children's television. Apparently, kids are actively choosing to watch Deal or No

Deal: to me, it's frankly amazing the show is popular with such a young audience. On occasion, it almost makes me feel slightly trendy.

Not long ago I was in a Bristol garage and the girl behind the counter said, 'I am so pleased your show is a hit.' Before I could answer, the chap standing behind me in the queue, said, 'Not half as pleased as he bloody is.' He was spot on. I am deliriously happy that Deal or No Deal is such a phenomenal success. I feel very grateful to be part of this amazing programme that somehow touches the hearts of people so deeply.

In addition to our fantastic viewing figures, we've also won some truly prestigious awards. Being awarded the Rose d'Or for the Best Game Show in Lucerne was fantastic. We were one of many global versions of Deal or No Deal in contention for the prize, yet we scooped this prestigious international award for our simple-yet-effective interpretation of the show. I was also thrilled to be nominated for a BAFTA in 2005, particularly since we had only been on air for two months. We've won 'Daytime Programme of the Year' at the Royal Television Society Awards and the TV Quick award for Best Daytime Programme. But now I just want to slow it all down. It's been a 'pinch-yourself' experience and I want time to enjoy and absorb everything that has happened.

Before season two of Deal or No Deal, producers Richard, Glenn and I sat and discussed whether to make any changes to the show to keep it fresh and the audience on their toes. It didn't take long for us to decide 'if it ain't broke, don't fix it'. The whole point of Deal or No Deal is that each player makes their show different and entirely their own. And that's what makes it compelling viewing for millions of people every day.

It's traditional in television for production teams to change and evolve with each series, but many of the key people returned for the second season of Deal or No Deal. I think that says a lot about the team, the atmosphere and the success of the show.

I feel sad because I wish Noel had won tonight. He does a tremendous job on Deal or No Deal. It's a brilliant format but what really makes it so watchable and so entertaining is Noel's presence.
Jonathan Ross at the BAFTA Awards, 2006

This book is a celebration of that success. It's designed to guide you through the highlights, the shocks and the frankly ridiculous moments of season one, giving you exclusive behind-the-scenes access. The nation has been addicted to following the many contestants, the cunning game-play and the nail-biting drama. I hope you enjoy reading about these experiences as much as I love being part of them.

And to think I nearly turned it down!

CHAPTER 2

Deal or No Deal spins around like a television windmill every 24 hours, pitching countless people behind red and blue boxes into green rooms, multi-coloured shirts and even into doing a 10.30 pm hokey cokey with age-defying enthusiasm. The day-to-day production of this extraordinary television show is far from routine, though it runs like clockwork thanks to the intense concentration and dedication of its intensely dedicated staff. But that's only part of the story. For the first time ever, we're delighted to present the true, in-depth behind-the-scenes happenings, just for those folks (like Noel) who appreciate some order in their cosmos...

24 HOURS IN THE LIFE OF DEAL OR NO DEAL

7.00 Studio unlocked. Vermin exterminated.

8.00 Cleaner arrives. Vermin hoovered. Runners arrive to check studio is in working order and vermin-free.

9.00 At the contestants' hotel, 22 alarms go off. 22 snooze buttons then pressed.

9.10 Contestants press snooze again.

10.00 Contestants arrive at breakfast complaining of slight/severe/debilitating hangovers. Studio technical check. Assistant producers arrive on site and begin daily checks on current contestants, arriving contestants and their guests. Edit producer Nick and line producer Julie arrive. Editors arrive complaining of slight/severe/debilitating hangovers.

10.30 Series producer Glenn Hugill and executive producer Richard Hague arrive.

10.35 Glenn Hugill and Richard Hague have tea break.

10.45 Glenn Hugill goes to edit suites to review the latest shows due for delivery to Channel Four. Checks shows for content, dramatic tension and loud swear words.

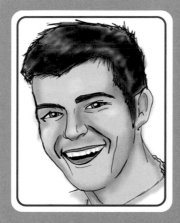

Name
Jim Connolly

Job
Assistant Producer, responsible for looking after the contestants

Best/Worst Moment

After months of preparation, we were finally in the studio ready to record our very first show. Twenty-two hopefuls stood lined up behind their boxes, the audience had taken their seats and Noel walked on to the floor. The atmosphere was tense as we moved to the big moment – who would be the first contestant chosen to take on The Banker?

Noel announced, 'And our first player is.... LYNN!'

The audience cheered, the contestants applauded, and out came...LEN!

'Yeeeeeessss!' he cried, doing a victory dance down the Walk of Wealth.

Lynn stopped in her tracks, the other contestants looked at each other in confusion – then the entire studio dissolved into whoops of laughter.

I walked on to the floor and made my way over to Len.

'Mate, it's not you, it's LYNN!' I said.

'Oh No,' he said, and made his way back to his place.

After the laughter died down, Lynn took her place at the pound table and we recorded a great first show.

It was a bizarre thing to happen on our first day but it was also my Best Moment because it broke the ice and really bonded everyone together.

10.50 Richard Hague has second tea break. Polishes awards.

11.00 Noel arrives to do interviews for radio and press, accompanied by his nutritionist, masseuse, stylist, Feng Shui consultant, bodyguards and Fifi, his chihuahua.

11.30 Production team meets with series producer to confirm the three contestants who will play that day. Any special requirements of the set or for contestants' guests are discussed. The identity of the day's contestants is kept a well-guarded secret from the contestants themselves.

11.50 Filming crew and director Richard van't Riet arrive.

12.00 Lunch served on site for production and camera crew.

12.30 Coach arrives at hotel with care assistant producer ('Care AP') to pick up contestants.

12.45 Contestants arrive at green room.

12.50 The 21 contestants left from the previous evening's record go straight into make-up and wardrobe. The new contestant entering the 22 is informed by the Care AP and he/she also goes into make-up and

wardrobe to complete the full 22 line-up. This is the longest period of preparation the contestants get during the day. During this period the contestants also select from the menu and they and their guests then eat lunch. Also at this time, contestants inform the care team if they have any more friends and family planning on heading down during their stay, so that appropriate arrangements can be made.

13.00 Hair and make-up and wardrobe crew take care of Noel and contestants. Contestants wear their own clothes but must be checked for colour clashes and 'strobing' – a

Name
Richard van't Riet

Job
Director. If the producers are the architects of the show I'm the builder. The director has to make sure the house is built with all the bits in the right place at the right time. So when the architects come back saying something isn't working...you have to fix it!

Best moment
When Morris Simpson said 'No deal' to £101,000...and then the look on his face for that split second when he realised he didn't have the £250,000 in his box!

Worst moment
The day catering decided to cook a BBQ on what, to this Australian, looked like a flame thrower. Or perhaps the night one of catering had a few too many to drink and declared he 'loved us all'...in the men's toilet! That was fairly memorable...

Name
Glenn Hugill

Job
Series Producer. In theory this means I have responsibility for all the creative content of Deal or No Deal. In practice it means I give a few incomprehensible instructions to the team; they go away and do brilliant work of their own design and I take all the credit.

Best moment
Genuinely, it's 10:30 am every single day that I come into work.

Worst moment
10:31 am.

Name
John Clarke

Job
Steadicam Operator

Best moment
I follow Noel around filming and one day when a contestant was dithering, he said, 'Come on, we're going for a walk.' We all dashed up to the end of the road, found someone riding a bike and asked them should the player Deal or No Deal? It was a very surreal moment!

Worst moment
Every Friday night at 9.30 pm. Noel takes the mickey out of me all week because I wear shorts and big boots that make me look like Noddy. But that rig is heavy. I carry around five or six stone in weight every day and by the end of the week I'm absolutely fried!

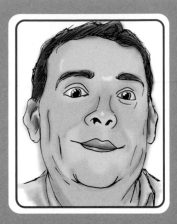

Name
Mark Olver

Job
Warm-up 'Artiste' (with an 'e' – it's classier)

Best moment
My mum lives in Bristol and one day she came to see the show. I was doing the warm-up, and as usual when Noel arrives on set, I stopped talking and told everyone to give him a cheer. This day, he storms on shouting, 'I'm not talking to you.'

'What on earth…?' I say, thinking wouldn't you know it, the one day my mum comes…

'You just blanked me,' shouts Noel across the set.

It transpired we were filling up our cars at the same petrol station that morning. Noel saw me and started waving and shouting 'Hi Mark,' like a loon across the forecourt – and I ignored him, which as you can imagine doesn't happen that often.

It was incredibly funny, especially when he started joshing my mum about how badly I'd been brought up and how truly awful my manners were…

Worst moment
It really gets to you when people lose. I always remember Fadil Osman, who'd recently had a family tragedy. He wrote what he hoped to win in Noel's book – and ended up in the 1p Club. When Noel opened the book afterwards, there was no amount written there, just a big, happy, smiley face. I remember thinking, yes, your priorities are right, you really know how to play this game. In homage for a while afterwards, we all went round saying, 'Fadil or No Fadil?'

problem some striped and checked clothes cause for TV cameras. Noel's shirts arrive in a specially sealed container in case they blind the postman.

13.05 Independent adjudicator arrives.

13.15 Director and series producer take their places in the gallery. Camera, sound and lighting check.

13.40 Studio assistant producer and floor manager collect contestants to enter the studio. Independent adjudicator loads the numbers in the boxes, which are then taken on set in a locked cage.

13.45 Contestants enter studio and take up the positions they were initially allocated as they entered the 22. The 22 boxes are in front of them on the studio walkway. They pick out one of 22 numbered balls at random from a bag and are handed the box corresponding to the number they have picked. They then take their position with their boxes for individual and line-up cutaway shots. It's a nervous time for all the players and they will often joke with each other to try and keep on top of their nerves. Most frequently it's the friendly banter about which of the two wings, East or West, is the greatest. East Wingers often claim that it's the most intelligent wing; the counter argument being simply that 'The West Wing is the best wing'.

13.50 Audience enters studio. Mark Olver, top warm-up man, arrives on set and gets contestants and audience in the mood. He is very funny at this point.

13.55 Banker arrives on site.

14.00 Banker takes up position in his office. Noel introduced on set and recording starts. Recording then begins and continues until the contestant selection has been revealed on the game board. The selected player is then led away to have a radio microphone attached, and any guests they have are given a 'mic' also. The next standby contestant is taken from the audience up to wardrobe and make-up ready to go straight in to the next recording session. This saves them having to rush around for their first time and once they're ready they can watch the show unfold in the viewing room with either the Care AP or researcher, depending on who's around.

14.00 – 16.00 Main show recording session. Recording occasionally lasts longer – up to two and a half hours depending on how a game unfolds. As always, anything can happen. The game may be a nightmare or a dream; the contestant may agonise

Name
Jane Atkinson

Job
Production Manager: looks after staffing, scheduling, budgets... the buck stops here!

Best Moment

Recently we took three boxes backstage to a show Noel was recording for Channel 4's T4. We were instantly mobbed by desperate celebs – Vernon Kay, Matt from Busted, a couple of Zutons, some actors from Hollyoaks – who wanted to know if these boxes were the real thing...

Worst moment

When contestant Joe Walvish fell ill and had to go to hospital. It was a very concerning time, but as soon as he was well enough, he came back and played his game.

Name
Richard Hague
Job
Executive Producer, overseeing all that is Deal or No Deal. Also purveyor of fine wines and cheap vodka.

Best moment
Seeing a contestant cry.

Worst moment
Running out of tissues because of the above.

Name
Mitch Silcock

Job
Art Department Assistant, creating the set and keeping the boxes safe and secure at all times

Best moment
The special Valentine's Day show. The set looked classy: we put swathes of red silk across the wings, heart icons on the boxes, and got everyone into evening dress and tuxedos.

Worst moment
Massimo Dimambro's show when the box was knocked to the floor. My heart jumped into my mouth in panic. Only three of us are authorised to touch the boxes, and we all ran on set. But this was unprecedented and we didn't have a clue what to do! In the end, the boxes had to be reset by the adjudicator, and the game went on.

Name
Michelle James

Job
Assistant Producer of the care team looking after the contestants

Best moment
When Gaz Hall won £100,000. I'd picked him at audition in Brighton, thinking he was lovely. He was quiet and unassuming, not a loud character, and during the game he had a tough time, so it was brilliant in the end when he did really well.

Worst moment
Nick Bain's a bit of a joker, and when he told his wife he'd only won 1p, she thought he was having her on. I had to call her and tell her it was true. She was gutted and burst into tears on the phone.

for hours or make their minds up instantly. Perhaps they'll go into the audience, backstage or even outside. No matter what happens during the game, Noel and the camera team will follow the action as it happens. And if necessary, Noel may fetch the Lucky Hat. Or indeed the Lucky Teabag (see Dictionary of Deal or No Deal, page 158). Every single player has a different game and every single player has a different approach. Some believe in destiny; some believe you make your own luck; many more simply think that 'whatever will be, will be'. Whether there's laughter or tears; big money or pocket change, Noel and the crew have learnt to expect the unexpected during these recordings.

16.00 Dinner. The contestants and crew eat in separate parts of the complex so as not to risk anyone finding out who is playing next.

16.45 Contestants are redressed in a second outfit and their make-up retouched. They arrive back on the studio floor and the boxes are loaded and selected at random as before. The procedure is much the same as before the first recording but now time is more pressing. (Contestants have approximately 15 minutes, depending on how quickly they get back from dinner

Name
Stephen Boodhun

Job
Producer

Best moment
When Morris Simpson was offered £101,000 by The Banker. It was a critical moment – he was on the cusp of winning £250,000 and I nearly exploded with anticipation.

Worst moment
When we lost power. The national grid was playing up and the whole of Bristol West came to a halt. Andrew Weir, an ex-soldier, was in the chair at the time, but we had to pack in the show and go to the pub instead.

Name
Adam MacDonald

Job
Head of daytime TV,
Channel 4

Worst moment
When Noel said no to presenting Deal or No Deal the
first time round.

Best moment
When we saw Noel do rehearsals in the Ministry of
Sound. He was immediately natural and brilliant. I was
there with my deputy Mark Downie, and five minutes in
we looked at each other and raised our eyes in delight.
Noel's performance instantly stepped the show up to
another level, and it was clear from that moment that
DOND could be a great success.

and whether or not they now have spaghetti carbonara in their eyebrows.) The selected player who has just played and therefore left the 22 will sign their winner's letter and expenses form in the green room during the next recording, and then watch the show in the viewing room with either the Care AP or researcher – but they are never left on their own! The new standby contestant takes their place in the 22.

16.50 Noel retrieved from his oxygen tank.

16.55 Second audience of the day arrives to be greeted by Mark Olver. He is slightly less funny in this record as he is a bit tired now, bless him.

17.00 Second recording session begins.

19.00 Half hour reset, new player brought in. Usual checks etc.

19.10 Noel has his aura cleansed and eats a ham sandwich.

19.30 Third shoot of the day. The audience is the same as for the second recording. The floor manager, Greg, does most of the warm-up here as Mark is now so tired he is usually asleep in his basket.

21.30 Contestants board the bus back to the hotel. Care AP accompanies them to ensure smooth check-in and greeting for any arriving 'newbies'. Party starts in the hotel bar.

22.00 Noel, Richard, Glenn et al. leave the building. To rapturous applause.

22.30 Contestants hokey cokey round the hotel lobby/street.

23.00 to midnight: Runners clear the studio for the night; checking for problems, breakages and, of course, vermin.

Name
Clayton Lonie Jr.

Job
Senior Editor

Best moment
Finding out the show was filming in Bristol, not London. That meant I could do a daily commute from Plymouth to Bristol – it's done wonders for my family life.

Worst moment
Finding out my wife was pregnant over the phone. It's the kind of thing a man would like to be told in person...

2.00 to 3.00 Contestants go to bed. Being on Deal or No Deal is a bit like freshers' week at university. No one wants to miss out on any of the excitement – everyone wants to get together, have fun and enjoy the experience to the full. But many contestants are in their 50s and upwards and don't have the stamina (or livers) of 18-year-old students. Nevertheless, they can often be found in the early hours at the party-to-end-all-parties, keeping up with even the youngest contestants.

A real bond forms in the wee small hours and most contestants make friendships that continue long after the show has finished. For many of them, this is what makes Deal or No Deal so incredibly special and why so many people call it 'the best time of their lives'.

4.00 to 7.00 Contestants attempt to sleep, regularly

Name
Jane Tooze

Job
DOND stylist and procurer of Noel's shirts (nasty job but someone's got to do it...)

Best moment
The ongoing buzz about Noel's shirts. We experimented with a few ideas but felt that keeping the look simple and having fun with patterns would be most interesting. I never cease to be amazed they create such a stir...

Worst moment
When lovely Lucy Harrington who'd been with us for 50 shows walked away with only a fiver.

interrupted by trips to the loo as their systems flush out the pints of water (and various other beverages) they downed before lights out to prevent hangovers (see 10.00 above).

Meanwhile, Noel dreams of re-arranging the cosmos.

Next Day The process begins again – just the same and yet totally different!

CHAPTER 3

He is a mysterious mastermind who controls each Deal or No Deal game, tempting and testing the courage of contestants from his (deluxe with ensuite) eyrie somewhere near the studio. The Banker – like the best James Bond villain – strikes fear and fascination in the hearts of millions. Yet he remains a riddle wrapped within an enigma. At first, The Banker spoke only with Noel, prompting various rumours, the most ridiculous of which was that he doesn't exist. After talking personally with contestants, that myth was blown: instead, some poor deluded fools conjectured it was Alan Sugar or Simon Cowell or possibly even George Osborne trying out the role as Chancellor of the Exchequer in case the Tories win the next election. Who knows? The Banker is fabulously discreet. Or was …

AN INTERVIEW WITH THE BANKER

Determined to uncover the truth, we sent our charmingly tenacious reporter to coax information from the Notorious Mr Big, first swiping his telephone number from Noel's bulging personal organiser. On the following pages is a transcript of their confidential telephone call on ...

INT. Hello?

BANKER. Ahoy.

INT. Is that The Banker?

BANKER. Who is this? Is it Noel?

INT. No I'm not Noel. I'm Jo. Could I...

BANKER. You don't sound like Noel.

INT. I'm not Noel. I'm calling on behalf of the author? She's writing a book.

BANKER. About me?

INT. About the show.

BANKER. But focusing on me?

INT. Well...

Banker hangs up. Interviewer redials.

BANKER. Yes?

INT. It's me again. Sorry, sir, I made a mistake. Yes, naturally the book is about you.

BANKER. Of course it is. In that case, yes; it is I, The Banker. How may I help you?

INT. I have many questions your public would like answered.

BANKER. Ah yes... they find me fascinating don't they? As do I. It's understandable. Fire away, young lady.

INT. Firstly; what is your real name?

BANKER. Colin.

INT. Really?

BANKER. No, not really. I'm toying with you. You sound nice.

INT. Oh... thank you. Er...Can't you tell me your real name?

BANKER. Agh, you're as persistent as a wine stain. But, perhaps I will indulge you... My real name is the one you see every day. That describes my every fibre. I may have been born with a different name but I always was and shall forever be, The

Banker. But you can call me what you wish, my dear.

INT. Right, okay, I'll bear that in mind. Now, could you tell me how old you are?

BANKER. I was born on May 12th under the Chinese sign of the Dragon. Appropriate, *n'est ce pas?* I was 12 pounds in weight with a ferocious appetite both for hard knowledge and warm milk. My mother informs me that when the midwife slapped my back at birth, in return I elbowed her in the throat.

INT. Goodness. Okay, er...could you just tell me how old you are?

BANKER. Tut. I hope you will not prove impertinent. Not when I'm beginning to warm to you.

INT. Okay, fine. How did you get the job as The Banker?

BANKER. I don't see it so much as a job; to me it's more of a calling. But I understand your drift. Put simply; there was an advertisement in the pages of the quality financial press. It read 'Brilliant mind required to crush dreams. Must have huge fortune, evil streak and own car.'

INT. I see. What is your office like?

BANKER. Fittingly sumptuous. The walls are lined with a selection of books from my home. I have three libraries at my main residence. One contains books regarding mathematics, risk assessment and advanced economics; the second is filled with volumes detailing human psychology, behavioural science and non-verbal communication; and the third houses my

collection of 19th-century adult French lithographs. My office also has a number of monitors so I can watch every detail of a game as it progresses and, of course, a large black telephone. As I have mentioned elsewhere, mine is identical to the one seen on screen, only rather than having a question mark on the dial, it simply reads 'Noel'. Perhaps, if you are very nice to me, I might allow you a little peek…

INT. Er…Which of the contestants has been your favourite?

BANKER. I feel a little *quid pro quo* would be appropriate at this time.

INT. Pardon?

BANKER. Well, my dear, here you are firing questions at me like balls from an automatic tennis machine and yet I am being granted nothing in return. I'd like to know a little about you.

INT. But this is not supposed to …

BANKER. How old are you?

INT. I'd rather not say. You might get cross.

BANKER. Is that so? And where are you from?

INT. Originally, do you mean?

BANKER. Ah yes. Thank you. You may continue with your questions now.

INT. Okay, but…I thought I had to answer

your questions first.

BANKER. As you did, my dear, perfectly clearly.

INT. I didn't say anything at all.

BANKER. *Au contraire.* You told me that you are a 29-year-old journalist, originally from Liverpool, now living and working in central London.

There is a slight pause.

INT. But …that's impossible…How…how do you know that?

BANKER. Simple. You are at great pains to sound mature and professional. Indeed, no one under the age of 25 would use the word 'goodness' as a natural expression of surprise. However you are aware that you are trying to sound older than you are, which is why you felt that if you were to tell me your real age of 29 I might react angrily thinking that you were lying to disguise your advancing years. Ergo you truly are 29 years old. Also, this 'work voice' on which you have toiled so hard has many clumsily raised and lengthened vowels. Plus you replied 'originally' to my enquiry as to where you came from. I believe when you first moved to London you felt it might help you to have a non-regional accent. The inconsistency of sibilance when you use the letter 'T', and the 'O' sound when you nervously use the word 'okay', lead me to believe the accent you are attempting to unlearn is a Liverpudlian one. I know you are a journalist or it would be unlikely you would be given the task of interviewing me for a printed medium and you are clearly living and working in central London because I can hear your office workmates in the background and I have caller display on my telephone.

INT. I…I see.

BANKER. I also know your name is Jo.

Another pause.

INT. How… could you… possibly know that?

BANKER. You told me yourself at the beginning of this conversation. You've simply forgotten about it.

INT. Er…I did? …I mean…right. Right …I did, yes. Well…er…

BANKER. Come on, Jo. Ask me another.

What a shame you have muddled your accent. There's really no need in the modern arena. I love a Scouse accent myself. So very musical.

INT. Okay. I mean...right. How many... er...I mean how much...

BANKER. Spit it out...

INT. (spluttering slightly) What is your estimated wealth?

BANKER. What an unseemly question. Let us just say...slightly more than Noel.

INT. I see. And how tall are you?

BANKER. I refer you to my last answer.

INT. Right, fine, and do you have staff?

BANKER. I do. I have my man, Pennyworth, and a driver, Harrison. I also have a masseur named André. He has magic hands. After a hard day spent lifting and replacing that receiver, he is a godsend to me, I can tell you. As I understand it, I also have a cook but I couldn't swear to it as I have never been in my kitchen.

INT. Do you spend any of your free time with Noel?

BANKER. No. We've met but we don't socialise. He's a very positive person, you see. I'm rather the opposite. And yet we fit very well on the telephone. Perhaps he is the Yang to my Yin.

INT. Which of the past contestants is your favourite?

BANKER. Ah yes. I've been considering this question since you first asked it. Now, I suspect you think I'm going to say the members of the 1p Club. But let me think. Buzz, Mally and Lofty were smashing. Pat M, she was great value, as was Pennie, ironically. The wonderful Stevie; my black widow. And of course the beautiful Audrey. Mmmmm. No, but I think, however, all in all, my absolute favourite was Marcus. And the members of the 1p Club.

INT. And your least favourite?

BANKER. Morris and Kirsty. They almost... that is to say they might have... taken my precious £250,000 away. And that Jennifer Miller. She'd better hope she doesn't meet me in a dark alley behind an expensive restaurant.

INT. Speaking of restaurants, what is your favourite meal?

BANKER. Liver. And fava beans. With a nice 1953 Chateau Lafite. And chips.

INT. How do you prepare for each show?

BANKER. André gives me a rub down while I check the markets.

INT. Who is your role model?

BANKER. So many... Freud, Einstein, Nietzsche, Shylock, David Cassidy, Vlad the Impaler, both Mr Kiplings, Goldfinger, Mozart, Johnny Weissmuller, Lex Luthor, ABBA and my Mother.

INT. What was your previous job?

BANKER. That's classified. Although I can tell you I am a qualified dentist.

INT. Is it difficult remaining anonymous in day-to-day life?

BANKER. Not at all. Despite my enormous fame and popularity I can move freely among the little people. A bit like the stars

of The Archers.

INT. What would you say to the people who continue to think that there is nobody on the end of the phone?

BANKER. I would tell them to put their life savings in an unmarked envelope and send them directly to me, care of the show. No need to include their name or address.

INT. According to *The Guardian* newspaper, you are 'a cult character in the making and no mistake'. How do you respond to this?

BANKER. I would very much hope that it wasn't a typo as I am very attracted to the idea of a cult. People pay to worship me...I like the premise.

INT. How do you spend your free time?

BANKER. Economically.

INT. Do you ever feel tempted to reveal your identity?

BANKER. I do reveal my identity. Indeed, I have done so in this interview. I. Am. The. Banker.

INT. Okay. Here's one all the ladies want to know. You have been known to flirt with some of the contestants... So...are you single?

BANKER. Ah ha. The position of Mrs Banker is currently vacant, yes. I have been married on six previous occasions. I have an easy rhyme I use to remind me what happened to each wife:

Divorced, divorced, divorced;
Divorced, beheaded, divorced.

INT. Beheaded?

BANKER. Next question please.

INT. Right. Next question... Okay, on the subject of rhymes, you often seem to prepare poems for the contestants. Why is this?

BANKER. I have always had a great love of verse. I like the order; the mathematic form. I wrote my first poem when I was only eight, you know. It was entitled 'Stuffing the Christmas Goose' and it went thusly:

My grandmama had a kitchen maid
Whose cooking I detested.
When she under-figged my pudding
I found reasons to have her arrested.

There is silence on the telephone line for a moment.

INT. How do you come up with your offers?

BANKER. I trust my instinct. Of course I use my knowledge of probabilities and risk but at the end of the day it comes down to me and the contestant. *Mano a mano.*

The greatest pleasure I receive is from getting someone to accept an offer that really should have been far higher to mathematically cover my risk. But that takes great courage and great trust in my ability to correctly identify someone's breaking point. And everyone is different. That's why I am unlikely to give the same offer in any two games even with identical amounts still in play. I want that box for as little money as possible. And to do that I'm prepared to take the occasional gamble.

INT. But that can backfire on you can't it? If you get it wrong.

BANKER. ....

INT. Hello?

BANKER. .... I suppose... some might say that. It's possible.

INT. Well, let's take Gaz's game, for example.

BANKER. Look I'm very busy right now...

INT. He was left with £10,000 and £100,000 and you only offered him £35,000. Surely if you'd offered, say £45,000 he would have taken it and you would have saved over 50 grand?

BANKER. I, I don't think, er...necessarily that...

INT. You misread him, didn't you? And it cost you big.

BANKER. Now, you listen to me. He got lucky. That's all. All those big winners. Lucky, lucky, lucky. I am a genius. I am undefeatable.

INT. Except when you get defeated.

BANKER. Well...... yes.

INT. Does it hurt you? When they beat you?

BANKER. .... Yes. Yes it does.

INT. How do you console yourself?

BANKER. Well... when I was little, Mummy would make me eggy bread yum yums when I was sad and so now Pennyworth will often.... er...wait. That's...that's enough of that. Wrap this interview up.

INT. Mr Banker. Thank you.

BANKER. Goodbye.

Hangs up.

From the time they get up (around 10 am) to the time they drop (don't ask), every minute in the life of a Deal or No Deal contestant is packed with drama, passion and rollercoaster extremes of emotion. Some say life on DOND is like a luxury holiday camp, others that it's akin to going on a school trip with your best mates. But what actually happens when you become a 'newbie' and enter the green room for the first time? We've asked a few contestants about their experiences on the show, from the moment they attend the auditions to the drama of their farewell speeches. There's one thing they all agree on: being on DOND is the best fun they've ever had...

A DAY IN THE LIFE OF...
THE CONTESTANT

THE AUDITION

Once an applicant is called to audition, the fun begins. Auditions are held at venues around the country, and the research team invites 20 or 30 applicants to take part. They're not looking for barnstormers and comedians, but varied and interesting personalities of all ages and backgrounds who are confident enough to be themselves. **Lee Hartland** left his audition thinking he wouldn't hear from the team again. 'There were some big, OTT characters there, so I was really surprised they picked me,' he said. Another contestant, **Russell Cook**, was waiting for his wife while she auditioned, and only agreed to go in to 'make up the numbers'. He, too, made it to the show. The 'auditionees' are often split into two teams, sometimes male/female, sometimes simply down the middle of the room. To loosen up they play charades, followed by games of chance. Pensioner **Nancy Englefield** rose to the team occasion with feisty toughness. 'I was in an all-women side against the men,' she said. 'The women had been losing consistently, so I was incredibly pleased to score for the girls when I went up!' Finally there's a speech to camera to see how people come across on the screen. Everyone is encouraged to talk a little about themselves for a minute or so. (Though actually, they often need very little encouragement).

NEWBIES

The ones that get the call experience an intense first day when they arrive at the DOND studios in Bristol West. The new contestants or 'newbies' will be welcomed into the bosom of the current game players, some of whom will be into their 20th or 30th game. Chaperoned by a crew member or 'care bear' as

Lee Hartland takes home
£50,000

Russell Cook takes home
£21,000

Nancy Englefield takes home
£18,500

they're known, the new kids are effectively handed over to their new family. 'All of a sudden, 22 people came into the green room all happy and chirpy and bubbly and bouncy,' says **Dave Woollin** of his first experience of the emotionally-charged moment after a show is filmed. Then it's off to wardrobe, to vet the outfits the new contestant has chosen and packed with care, avoiding tops that 'strobe' (go all squiggly) on camera (or, more likely, clash with Noel's). The wardrobe mistress confiscates the clothes allocated for each show, and the seizing of said items has been known to cause minor fluctuations in the local economy as serious shoppers head to the high street to replenish their wardrobes.

The newbie then sits as an audience member before their first game inside the 22, to prevent that unique 'rabbit caught in camera lights' look of the DOND virgin. Once they've got the hang of things, they join the game and are introduced to Noel. After the day's shooting is over, they all pile in the bus and are driven back to the hotel. That night is a baptism of fire as the overwhelmed and emotional newbie begins to find out what they've let themselves in for. **Lucy Harrington** spent her arrival evening 'bonding'. 'I stayed up to get to know all these different people of different backgrounds and ages,' said Lucy. 'We all got very drunk...' As the longest-serving contestant with 50 shows under her belt, that rip-roaring night was doubtless the first of many.

THE HOTEL

The contestants all stay in the same hotel not far from the studios. Each of the rooms is a twin-bed as everyone is invited to bring along a guest for support. Many bring mothers or husbands and wives. 'The guests become as much of a part of the group as the contestants themselves,' says **Marcus Neill**, swelling the party numbers to more like 40 than 22. Making sure that the contestants are happy in this environment is of great importance and representative 'daddy' and 'mummy' contestants are assigned to look after the group, welcoming newbies and liaising between contestants and the Care APs (assistant producers). In this luxury environment – 'better than the best holiday I've had,' said **Dave Ellis** – contestants are well looked after. In the mornings, **Morris Simpson** used to have breakfast at nine, go to the sauna for 20 minutes, the steam room for 20 minutes, have a swim in the pool, then end up in the jacuzzi. Marcus claims he piled on at least a stone in his time there, owing to the cooked breakfasts. 'I did go into the gym once. I managed five minutes on the exercise bike, then went back to bed.'

STANDING IN THE WINGS

Three shows are filmed a day but every DOND is as unique as Noel, the team and The Banker give a fresh and fuelled performance each time. Contestants remain in their opening position throughout their stay, and there's gentle rivalry between the 11 players on each 'Wing'. Like football teams, they bait each other and boast their brilliance to keep morale high. Veteran DOND-er Lucy was in the East Wing. 'We rocked,' she said with unabashed bias. 'We might not have been as beautiful as the West Wing but we were feistier. They were hot, but we were cool!'
For a time, a dance competition emerged with more and more outlandish and experimental boogying going on unseen by viewers during the rolling titles. But the production team got concerned when contestants began the show flushed and out-of-breath. The dance was banned when an unnamed retired member attempted an old-

Dave Wollin takes home
£20,000

Lucy Harrington takes home
£5

Marcus Neil takes home
£31,000

Dave Ellis takes home
1p

Morris Simpson takes home
£20,000

school head spin during a break-dancing session, and health and safety fainted clean away.

The players choose their boxes by drawing a numbered ping pong ball from a bag. It's random, but that doesn't stop contestants feeling they've brought good or bad luck with them for the player who's taking main stage. One day Dave Woollin unknowingly had the Big One in his box. '**Simon Cowley** selected that box at a very pivotal moment and I will forever feel guilty. The feeling you get when you open up the £250k for someone is awful. It makes you feel genuinely sick.' Marcus loved getting his number picked 'because it meant the camera was on me!' Noel strikes up a quirky chemistry with each contestant while they're in the Wings and thought Morris Simpson had a totally fresh approach. 'He'd respond only in rhyme particularly before he opened a box,' he said. 'He was determined for the audience to remember him.' The DOND laureate's first ditty went: 'Box 22, I hope it's a blue just for you...' and Morris 'the Poet' was born.

HOKEY COKEY!

After a hard day's filming the contestants and guests usually stagger back into the hotel as late as 10 pm and for quite a few, it's a case of a nightcap. Or ten. During which time daddy/mummy will conduct speeches, introducing the newbies and the day's winners, who each make a leaving speech. The departing member sometimes hands out cards and often passes round a book for everyone to sign and add contact details so that they can stay in touch with everyone.

Then, at 10.30 pm, a nightly ritual is performed. The dance of the hokey cokey, and in particular the wail of 'shake it all about' is believed, after several pints of strong lager, to be a wealth-inducing mantra, and has been known to spill out into the street, sweeping up in its wake a couple of policeman and a nearby wedding party. 'It's the most enormous fun', says Lucy Harrington.

According to many, the hotel staff are as much an extension of the DOND 'family' as the contestants and crew. Which is just as well considering how seriously some of the members party. 'About four of us would stay up every night till six or seven in the morning,' confessed Marcus Neill. 'There was one time I fell asleep in the lift, sitting in **Beryl Urquhart's** wheelchair.' (We have been assured Beryl is not pursuing a charge.) 'We'd get to the studios and the crew would be smirking, "Ooh, I heard about you last night!"' he adds, bashfully.

Simon Cowley takes home
£250

Beryl Urquhart takes home
£21,000

Nancy Englefield takes home
£18,500

WHAT GAME PLAN?

With any wildly successful game show, methodological theories and myths abound, and DOND is no exception. Contestants are very reluctant to believe that no external factors influence the box's contents, and game plans and strategies concerning the concepts of fate, lucky numbers, probability, star signs or indeed alien intervention are off- and on-screen obsessions. One contestant used the numbers of her favourite dishes in her local Chinese restaurant. Another was convinced he'd cracked a mathematical code or 'grid' system to which the box numbers conformed. (His first three choices turned out to be big reds, blowing that theory out of the water.) Yet another used 4 and multiples of 4 in her choices, and walked away with a respectable £46,000. One good wheeze is to play a psychological game and pit your wits against The Banker – a tactic that always gives Noel a great deal of joy. '**Gary Owen** was the first person to play Bluff the Banker,' guffaws Noel in sweet memory of the moment. 'He'd planned it all beforehand and it was a brilliant bit of game play. He told The Banker what his "aim" was (£30,000), and of course the Banker took the bait and offered him £29,999. Gary quickly accepted as he'd actually only wanted half of that!' It was ingenious but the Banker is wise to this type of trickery now, so Gary was both the first and last player to lead him so spectacularly astray.

IN THE CHAIR

After a couple of weeks, most contestants have a feeling that the spotlight will soon land on them. Though, as Lucy's case showed – she waited 50 games for her turn! – nothing in the DOND universe is ever predictable. Lucy loved the experience so much she didn't actually want to play. 'There's a pattern for most people: the first ten shows, they think "I'm not ready", but by the time they get to 18/20 shows they're like, "I'm ready, stick me in the chair, let's get this over now, it's just tormenting me!" I just wasn't like that, I wanted to stay for ever.' The chosen player is immediately swamped with good luck wishes from the other contestants, but gets a moment or two to compose themselves while they're miked up. Some contestants are calm, others nervous, but all say the show races past – two hours seems like ten minutes. A few contestants purposefully make fairly quick decisions, as the pressure is great. Others, such as **Sue Hopper** who says she took 'aaaaaages', admit that their game went on much, much longer than

Noel's Tips to be a Top Contestant!

When you take the Walk of Wealth towards that 'Crazy Chair', here's how to make sure your game is remembered for all the right reasons!

1 POSITIVE ATTITUDE

We want every player to make the most of their one-off occasion by staying optimistic, whatever the boxes throw at them! The most positive players encourage a huge amount of support from their fellow contestants and the audience, and it's a pleasure to be part of their experience.

2 CHARISMA

Physical appearance is not important – the personality and character of a player is what gets the audience on your side. Charismatic and entertaining players are inspiring to watch and immediately get everyone rooting for them.

3 FOCUS

It's easy to get distracted by other contestants, the audience and the television crew. But if your focus wavers, you'll start making silly mistakes – such as becoming incapable of counting to three or forgetting what the offer was! These are signs of distraction The Banker leaps on with glee, and your offers will suffer as a result. Stay focused: this is your game!

4 COURAGE

It can all go horribly wrong. We've seen tears, shock and regrets, but the players who command the most respect are the ones who keep their nerve and bravely look forward, however nasty the situation they find themselves in.

the final edit suggests. The tension is palpable: everyone remembers the classic DOND moment in Morris's game: offered a staggering £101,000, he showed immense courage when he turned it down to chase the £250,000. 'That was a very tough decision - I've got two kids and £101,000 would change my life. But I wanted to be famous, the first person to win £250,000.' His decision took that extra bit of bravery and guts. The audience are crucial to the support and atmosphere of the game. Many contestants invite parents or spouses as guests and they are often asked their opinions – Noel calls it the 'swccp' – about whether the player should 'Deal' or 'No deal'. Every box that's opened elicits gasps of joy, relief or pity and the atmosphere is palpable. Noel often chats with the guests in the audience and Marcus livened up his game by joining the audience and taking over the role of host, asking Mr Edmonds, 'What brings you to The Marcus Show? Is it drugs or a paternity test?' à la Jerry Springer. Says Noel, 'I always tell the players, "It's your Channel 4; your game; your show," but nobody has ever taken me quite as literally as Marcus.'

GOING HOME

As with all good things, DOND must, for each contestant, come to an end. However, the evening after their game, the three exiting players go back to the hotel for their last night, to make their goodbye speeches, dance a final hokey cokey and celebrate until the early hours.

Joyfully reunited with friends and family, the ex-contestant is now a member of a club, with strong friendships with other players. There are websites for contestants to tell their experiences and help them stay in touch, there are reunions and invites to weddings, parties and holidays. On Dave Woollin's site, 270 contestants have signed up, posting over 18,000 messages. 'It's created something I never thought possible and long may it continue,' he says.

Everyone agrees that DOND is like no other experience and many say that going on the show is the best thing they ever did. Marcus Neill was in an airport flying home to Ireland less than 24 hours after his win. 'I looked at all these people going about their business and I wanted to jump up and down on the seats and scream, "You don't realise what's just happened to me!"'

To keep the suspense and tension of the programme, former contestants are encouraged to tell only a few close family or friends the result of their game. Many choose to keep it a complete secret and throw a party for the screening, so the outcome is only revealed then. As soon as the show is broadcast, contestants say people come up to them wherever they go – even in the gents' urinals, as **Gary 'Gaz' Hall** one day found out.

Whether you win big money or not, Deal or No Deal is a life-changing experience and leaving the show is for many a new beginning, not an end. As **Mally Welburn** said: 'All my life I've been up and down like a window cleaner, but the show put me on a new path, a new journey, and now the future's bright. Being on DOND was the best experience I've ever had.'

Sue Hopper takes home
£8,401

Gary Owen takes home
£29,999

Gary Hall takes home
£100,000

Mally Welburn takes home
£54,000

They're the meat in the Deal or No Deal sandwich, the cream in our coffee, the yin to our yang. They go to bed in the wee small hours and sleep as late as they can. They are the reason we love making this show, they are the tops. They are – the contestants!

There have been 234 of them in the first record-breaking, award-winning series of Deal or No Deal. Some have gone away with life-changing amounts, others have taken the penny, joining the no-less exclusive ranks of the 1p Club. Every contestant enters a battle of nerves, bravery, risk and reward, relying on gut instinct, personality and sheer luck to see them through. Their courage is indisputable, their passion and determination, awesome. They are, in short, the fuel in the Deal or No Deal tank, the '*bon*' to our Noel! We're proud to present their finest moments...

CHAPTER 5

THE WALK
OF WEALTH

1

CONTESTANT

Name Lynn Atherton
Broadcast 31st October 2005

THE GAME

Starting box No 15, containing £10
Banker offers £1,700, £900, £2,900, £2,900, £4,300, £14,000
Swap or no swap? No swap
Deal or No Deal? Deal!

Lynn takes home £14,000

2

CONTESTANT

Name Mark Grant
Broadcast 1st November 2005

THE GAME

Starting box No 6, containing £500
Banker offers £900, £1,500, £6,000, £8,500, £5,000, £9,900
Swap or no swap? No swap
Deal or No Deal? Deal!

Mark takes home £9,900

The highest total payout in a single week was £172,550. The lowest total payout in a single week was £39,364.02

3

CONTESTANT

Name Anita Wallas
Broadcast 2nd November 2005

THE GAME

Starting box No 21, containing £750
Banker offers £2,900, £4,000, £11,500, £22,000, £33,000
Swap or no swap? No swap
Deal or No Deal? Deal!

Anita takes home £33,000

DID YOU KNOW?

Left-handed contestants have won **52%** more money on average than right-handed contestants

---

4

CONTESTANT

Name Rachel Nkere-Uwem
Broadcast 3rd November 2005

THE GAME

Starting box No 10, containing £25,000
Banker offers £2,100, £1,500, £6,900, £8,400, £25,000
Swap or no swap? No swap
Deal or No Deal? Deal!

Rachel takes home £25,000

5

CONTESTANT

Name Haleem Khan
Broadcast 4th November 2005

THE GAME

Starting box No 17, containing £35,000
Banker offers £1,400, £4,500, £7,900, £18,500
Swap or no swap? No swap
Deal or No Deal? Deal!

Haleem takes home £18,500

6

CONTESTANT

Name Oliver Pitt
Broadcast 5th November 2005

THE GAME

Starting box No 3, containing £5,000
Banker offers £1,100, £5,200, £18,000, £4,000, £7,500, £8,000
Swap or no swap? No swap
Deal or No Deal? No deal

Oliver takes home £5,000

Cheese and onion is the most popular crisp flavour among contestants

7

CONTESTANT

Name Dilys Markwell
Broadcast 7th November 2005

THE GAME

Starting box No 7, containing £1,000
Banker offers £800, £3,200, £2,200, £3,500, £7,000
Swap or no swap? No swap
Deal or No Deal? Deal!

Dilys takes home £7,000

8

CONTESTANT

Name Paul Kelly
Broadcast 8th November 2005

THE GAME

Starting box No 19, containing 50p
Banker offers £1,300, £2,900, £700, £4,900, £6,500
Swap or no swap? No swap
Deal or No Deal? Deal!

Paul takes home £6,500

9

CONTESTANT

Name Michelle Worthington
Broadcast 9th November 2005

THE GAME

Starting box No 20, containing £20,000
Banker offers £4,300, £2,300, £6,600, £13,000, £19,900, £7,500
Swap or no swap? No swap
Deal or No Deal? Deal!

Michelle takes home £7,500

CONTESTANT
Name Natalie Gravillis
Broadcast 10th November 2005

THE GAME
Starting box No 9, containing £250,000
Banker offers £3,100, £1,700, £10,500, £22,000
Swap or no swap? No swap
Deal or No Deal? Deal!

Natalie takes home £22,000

CONTESTANT
Name Maurice Cheshire
Broadcast 11th November 2005

THE GAME
Starting box No 20, containing 50p
Banker offers £3,900, £7,100, £6,500, £13,000, £35,000
Swap or no swap? No swap
Deal or No Deal? Deal!

Maurice takes home £35,000

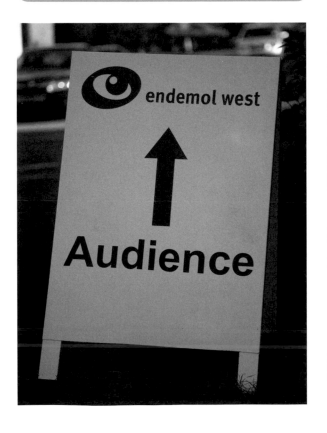

CONTESTANT
Name Lyndsey Young
Broadcast 12th November 2005

THE GAME
Starting box No 15, containing £10,000
Banker offers £800, £2,700, £9,000, £15,500
Swap or no swap? No swap
Deal or No Deal? Deal!

Lyndsey takes home £15,500

13

CONTESTANT
Name Adrienne Holt
Broadcast 14th November 2005

THE GAME
Starting box No 6, containing £1
Banker offers £1,100, £7,100, £9,500, £8,300
Swap or no swap? No swap
Deal or No Deal? Deal!

Adrienne takes home £8,300

14

CONTESTANT
Name Dr Madie Bolourchi
Broadcast 15th November 2005

THE GAME
Starting box No 6, containing £1
Banker offers £6,900, £1,600, £4,800, £28,000, £4,800
Swap or no swap? No swap
Deal or No Deal? Deal!

Madie takes home £4,800

15

CONTESTANT
Name Jan Thomson
Broadcast 16th November 2005

THE GAME
Starting box No 20, containing £1
Banker offers £2,100, £7,500, £13,300, £24,900
Swap or no swap? No swap
Deal or No Deal? Deal!

Jan takes home £24,900

DID YOU KNOW?

15% of contestants describe themselves as pessimists

16

CONTESTANT
Name Jayne Hill
Broadcast 17th November 2005

THE GAME
Starting box No 14, containing £5
Banker offers £500, £1,500, £2,500, £2,000, £4,000, £1,000
Swap or no swap? No swap
Deal or No Deal? Deal!

Jayne takes home £1,000

17

Ex-teacher **Jennifer Miller** kept cool under intense pressure to become Deal or No Deal's biggest winner in the first series, taking home £120,000! Read her story overleaf.

18

CONTESTANT
Name Elaine Bailey
Broadcast 19th November 2005

THE GAME
Starting box No 13, containing 10p
Banker offers £1,400, £2,100, £900, £3,000, £3,500
Swap or no swap? No swap
Deal or No Deal? Deal!

Elaine takes home £3,500

19

CONTESTANT
Name Leigh Tindsley
Broadcast 21st November 2005

THE GAME
Starting box No 1, containing £5
Banker offers £600, £6,000, £7,500, £2,500, £3,600
Swap or no swap? No swap
Deal or No Deal? Deal!

Leigh takes home £3,600

THE WALK OF WEALTH

PERSONAL FILE

Name
Jennifer Miller

Broadcast
18th November 2005

Occupation
Ex-teacher

Star sign
Capricorn

Eye colour
Brown

Favourite number
13

Crisp flavour
Plain

Favourite tipple
Red wine or Guinness

BANKER'S VERDICT

My nemesis. She found the courage to refuse over £50,000 and shook me to my very core. Indomitable. Sometimes, late at night, I see her face…

BEFORE THE SHOW

'I'd had the worst few years of my life. I'd had a long dark clinical depression which had started to shift – instead of a black sky it was sunshine and heavy cloud alternating. I hadn't been able to work so I'd been on benefits for the first time in my life. I'd accumulated debts of £38,000 and was struggling to make ends meet. I never watch daytime television but one day I was making a cup of tea and thought I'd switch it on – and saw the ad for Deal or No Deal. Fate was at work! If I could clear part of the debt, I'd feel better, and spending up to a month in a hotel in Bristol with new people might help me get unstuck. I was nervous – I'd been a recluse for ages – but it was a fantastic experience.

'Before the game, I tried to programme my mind to go for the blue boxes by doing affirmations like: "I only choose small blue amounts". I'm a trained counsellor and I think that really helped.'

THE GAME

'I completely used my intuition and let the boxes attract me. I focused on the numbers, not the people, and suddenly one would appear brighter. It was going well and I'd never felt so calm in my life: I thought, just let this flow. I was drawn to boxes 14 and 20, and didn't know which to choose, but then came certainty that the jackpot was in box 20. That was my guardian angel time!

'At the beginning of the game, I'd written my exit amount of £50,000 in Noel's book, so when The Banker offered me £52,000 I had a big internal debate. I was ready to deal, but when I opened my mouth "No deal" somehow came out. Like Noel, I'm an analytical, businesslike Capricorn, but I have Sagittarius rising and that's the madcap gambler of the horoscope. Then The Banker offered £120,000, and I said to Noel, you know what I have to do now. His eyes widened with horror. "Deal!" I said, and he breathed a sigh of relief. That night I had such an adrenalin rush I could hardly sleep.'

Starting box
No 9, containing
£750

Blues cruise 2

Red run 3

Banker offers
£2,300, £6,100,
£14,500, £33,000,
£52,000,
£120,000

Swap or no swap?
No swap

Deal or No Deal?
Deal!

Jennifer takes home £120,000

NOEL'S VERDICT

'Jennifer had her own aura. She was brilliantly positive whilst hiding the secret of how much the money meant to her. If The Banker had found out how much she needed the money, then his offers would have gone through the floor. They didn't: they went through the roof!'

BACK TO REAL LIFE

What's the first thing you did when you got home?
'I thought I'd kill myself if I drove home, so I booked into the best hotel in Bristol and stayed in bed for 24 hours.'

What did you do with the money?
'I cleared my debts which was absolutely wonderful. Gave my son a small gift – he wouldn't accept more – bought a new hatchback, treated my mum and close family to lunch on the Orient Express for her 85th birthday, and booked a holiday in the Maldives with my son and daughter-in-law. The rest is tucked away.'

Was the show life-changing?
'I feel much more balanced and relaxed about life. Before I had a very pessimistic outlook, I thought I was being left out of all the good stuff. But now this incredible thing has happened to me and it's as if the universe is saying, change your world view and be positive.'

Any advice?
'Ask for the best possible outcome and trust. Anything is possible – just look at me!'

20

CONTESTANT
Name Len Clarke
Broadcast 22nd November 2005

THE GAME
Starting box No 3, containing £50
Banker offers £3,200, £1,500, £1,900, £2,700, £9,400
Swap or no swap? No swap
Deal or No Deal? Deal!

Len takes home £9,400

21

CONTESTANT
Name Lisa Harris
Broadcast 23rd November 2005

THE GAME
Starting box No 9, containing £10
Banker offers £1,300, £5,200, £2,000, £8,100, £17,800
Swap or no swap? No swap
Deal or No Deal? Deal!

Lisa takes home £17,800

22

Mally Welburn from Hull was Deal or No Deal's second big winner, taking home £54,000 after a nailbiting, edge-of-the-seat show, and entering the Hall of Fame. Read his story overleaf.

23

CONTESTANT
Name Trevor Walker
Broadcast 25th November 2005

THE GAME
Starting box No 3, containing £1
Banker offers £3,100, £12,600, £4,900, £17,000, £47,000
Swap or no swap? No swap
Deal or No Deal? Deal!

Trevor takes home £47,000

14

Vegetarian contestants have won **31%** more money on average than those who eat meat. Jennifer Miller, the biggest winner of the series with **£120,000**, is a vegetarian

Contestants who don't drink tea or coffee have won **£33,463** on average, while tea drinkers have won **£16,840** and coffee drinkers **£13,858**

24

CONTESTANT
Name Sam Crompton
Broadcast 26th November 2005

THE GAME
Starting box No 10, containing £10
Banker offers £500, £4,000, £9,000, £16,500, £6,500, £2,100
Swap or no swap? No swap
Deal or No Deal? Deal!

Sam takes home £2,100

25

CONTESTANT
Name Rebecca Small
Broadcast 28th November 2005

THE GAME
Starting box No 1, containing £10
Banker offers £4,100, £8,200, £24,000, £20,000
Swap or no swap? No swap
Deal or No Deal? Deal!

Rebecca takes home £20,000

THE WALK OF WEALTH

PERSONAL FILE

Name
Mally Welburn

Broadcast
24th November 2005

Occupation
Fence and shed builder

Star sign
Taurus

Eye colour
Brown

Favourite number
13

Crisp flavour
Cheese and onion

Favourite tipple
Orange juice

BANKER'S VERDICT

'It takes a real gentleman to admit when he was wrong. I believe myself to be such a gentleman. Thus am unafraid to admit that I misread Mally completely. I thought I could get him for peanuts. A critical mistake. It won't happen again.'

BEFORE THE SHOW

'For a few years before, I'd been pursuing my dream of building fantasy sheds, done up inside as football teams' dressing rooms. But it went badly, badly wrong and I was on my uppers, living in a derelict building on my Jack Jones – apart from the rats. It was that bad they were coming to cut off the electricity when I saw a note about a new game show, and thought I've got to go for this. To be honest, I was more interested in the three hot meals a day than winning a big lot of money. I borrowed £100 from my daughter to buy some charity shop clothes for the show – they said you needed three changes a day. I did 14 shows and I was buzzing all the time. I couldn't sleep I was that hyped up. It was fantastic in that hotel, like being at a big wedding with all your friends, with all the grub you want, and all the time I never had nought in my pocket.'

THE GAME

'When my name flashed up, I felt I had the big boy in my box – and I was right. It was as if something was shining down on me: I'd got box 18 twice on the trot that day and my mother died on the 18th. At first I treated the game like a pack of cards: don't look at the board, you get trapped by it, just treat it like a set of odds. Then I changed it and went for the people who had a high number on the last show, because I don't believe you can get the same amount twice. It was working, I started to roll, I could feel myself twitch and sweat. The offer suddenly jumped to £54,000 and I had five boxes left. Five years ago I'd have got my gambler's head on and gone to the end. But everyone was saying, don't gamble, take the money now – they knew the situation I was in. I thought: would I take £54,000 out of my bank account and bet on these odds? The answer was no – so I dealt. I was gutted when we did the proveout round and I had the £250,000 after all. But you do the best you can and to me it was incredible to win that much money.'

NOEL'S VERDICT

'This was a brilliant game. Mally's an ex-deep sea trawlerman with a wonderful personality that made him a very popular player. I was not alone in being absolutely thrilled for him when he won such a huge sum of money. He deserved it!'

Starting box
No 18, containing £250,000

Blues cruise 3

Red run 5

Banker offers
£3,300, £2,300, £6,900, £6,900, £54,000

Swap or no swap?
No swap

Deal or No Deal?
Deal!

Mally takes home £54,000

BACK TO REAL LIFE

What's the first thing you did when you got home?
'I whopped the pillow for a couple of days. I'd been on such a high, pumped up with adrenalin, that afterwards I was flat as a pancake and I needed sleep to get me back up.'

What did you do with the money?
'I paid off my debts of about £8,000, gave my daughters £5,000 apiece, got myself a bedsit to live in. I didn't go on holiday or buy flash gear. I've invested in myself – I've paid £20,000 to have my autobiography published, and the returns are already coming in. I might not have won the £250,000 but I always say I'm going to be the first person on Deal or No Deal to make a quarter million from their winnings.'

Was the show life-changing?
'It's changed my life for the better and put me on another path. For me, the game wasn't just about opening boxes. It stopped me sleeping in a box.'

Any advice?
'Enjoy the experience. If you get a big offer, think about what that money could do to change your life. So many people chase it and lose it all...'

PERSONAL FILE

Name Raj Ahmed
Broadcast 29th November 2005
Occupation IT support analyst
Star sign Leo
Eye colour Brown
Favourite number 1
Favourite tipple Tequila

26

"My aim was to go travelling round Asia and Australia, pay off my debts and not think about work for a while. So when I saw the Deal or No Deal ad to win £250,000 it seemed too great an opportunity to miss. I played 25 shows, and the atmosphere was like a holiday camp. People were coming away with big sums – the smallest before me had been £1,000. None of us had any fear we'd go away empty-handed!"

THE GAME

"My plan was to avoid the people who regularly got big number boxes, but on the day they popped into my head first, and I picked them! I'm a gambler, and when it started going wrong, I kept pushing because I didn't want to give The Banker the satisfaction of settling for a low deal. When I finally opened my box with 10p, I felt sick. Completely numb. Even Noel didn't know what to say. All the contestants were devastated – it was a bit of a wake-up call. That night, everyone did a whip round for me, which was fantastic. But it was a bad day, and I always joke I've only just got over it."

Starting box No 3, containing 10p
Blues cruise 4
Red run 3
Banker offers £3,000, £7,200, £1,300, £4,000, £2,000, £200
Swap or no swap? No swap
Deal or No Deal? No deal

Raj takes home 10p

27

CONTESTANT

Name Andy Kelly

Broadcast 30th November 2005

THE GAME

Starting box No 22, containing £750

Banker offers £5,000, £10,000, £15,000, £9,000, £20,000

Swap or no swap? No swap

Deal or No Deal? Deal!

Andy takes home £20,000

28

CONTESTANT

Name Rita Ogunlana

Broadcast 1st December 2005

THE GAME

Starting box No 3, containing £75,000

Banker offers £1,100, £4,400, £2,800, £14,000, £29,000, £31,500

Swap or no swap? No swap

Deal or No Deal? Deal!

Rita takes home £31,500

DID YOU KNOW?

Contestants who describe themselves as pessimists have been the least successful!

29

CONTESTANT

Name James Roe

Broadcast 2nd December 2005

THE GAME

Starting box No 2, containing £10

Banker offers £5,500, £9,200, £5,000, £5,500, £17,600, £40

Swap or no swap? No swap

Deal or No Deal? No deal

James takes home £10

30

CONTESTANT

Name John Long

Broadcast 3rd December 2005

THE GAME

Starting box No 10, containing £35,000

Banker offers £2,100, £11,200, £3,400, £16,000

Swap or no swap? No swap

Deal or No Deal? Deal!

John takes home £16,000

31

CONTESTANT

Name Hayley Jones

Broadcast 5th December 2005

THE GAME

Starting box No 2, containing £10,000

Banker offers £700, £1,800, £7,400, £9,500, £18,200

Swap or no swap? No swap

Deal or No Deal? Deal!

Hayley takes home £18,200

32

CONTESTANT

Name Eddie Bond

Broadcast 6th December 2005

THE GAME

Starting box No 10, containing £250

Banker offers £1,000, £4,100, £7,200, £8,600, £10,100

Swap or no swap? No swap

Deal or No Deal? Deal!

Eddie takes home £10,100

33

CONTESTANT
Name Sarah Khan
Broadcast 7th December 2005

THE GAME
Starting box No 19, containing £100,000

Banker offers £6,300, £9,800, £20,000, £31,000

Swap or no swap? No swap

Deal or No Deal? Deal!

Sarah takes home £31,000

34

CONTESTANT
Name Tina Forster-Hill
Broadcast 8th December 2005

THE GAME
Starting box No 6, containing £5,000

Banker offers £1,200, £4,000, £2,000, £6,000, £1,700, £2,000

Swap or no swap? No swap

Deal or No Deal? No deal

Tina takes home £5,000

35

CONTESTANT
Name Kayode Allen-Taylor
Broadcast 9th December 2005

THE GAME
Starting box No 21, containing £100

Banker offers £9,000, £900, £6,600, £4,600, £7,500

Swap or no swap? No swap

Deal or No Deal? Deal!

Kayode takes home £7,500

Spirit drinkers have won more on average than wine and beer drinkers

36

CONTESTANT
Name Elaine Hoggarth
Broadcast 10th December 2005

THE GAME
Starting box No 16, containing £100,000
Banker offers £700, £3,000, £9,700, £12,000
Swap or no swap? No swap
Deal or No Deal? Deal!

Elaine takes home £12,000

37

CONTESTANT
Name Audrey Mulholland
Broadcast 12th December 2005

THE GAME
Starting box No 3, containing 1p
Banker offers £300, £1,200, £4,700, £2,300, £7,000, £8,500
Swap or no swap? No swap
Deal or No Deal? Deal!

Audrey takes home £8,500

Beer drinkers have won less money on average than non-drinkers and wine and spirit drinkers

PERSONAL FILE

38

Name Rob Appleyard
Broadcast 13th December 2005
Occupation Communications specialist
Star sign Pisces
Eye colour Blue
Favourite number 3
Crisp flavour Cheese and onion
Favourite tipple Malibu and coke (but does drink beer!)

"I was on the show for the experience, not the money, and it was the experience of a lifetime. There was such a good buzz about it. I played on my 28th show. It was Monday. I wasn't nervous, but I do remember this brief feeling of sadness when I walked up to the chair because it was the end of the journey – once you've played the game, you say your goodbyes."

THE GAME

'I loved being in that chair. It's my nature to play to the audience with stupid puns and bad jokes, and I kept the banter going with Noel until the end. I had a rubbish run, but it didn't matter. The £10,000 was great – we went on three holidays and did some garden improvements. But the most surreal moment was when I heard Ricky Gervais talking about Deal or No Deal on the radio, saying that my show was his favourite of all! To have someone that successful and funny enjoy it just added to the whole experience."

Starting box No 9, containing £10,000
Blues cruise 7
Red run 4
Banker offers £1,000, £500, £1,400, £1,000, £3,800, £11,000
Swap or no swap? No swap
Deal or No Deal? No deal

Rob takes home £10,000

39

CONTESTANT

Name Joanne Hornsby
Broadcast 14th December 2005

THE GAME

Starting box No 6, containing £11,000

Banker offers £1,300, £4,600, £11,200, £19,000

Swap or no swap? No swap

Deal or No Deal? Deal!

Joanne takes home £19,000

40

CONTESTANT

Name Jason Bailey
Broadcast 15th December 2005

THE GAME

Starting box No 2, containing 50p

Banker offers £7,000, £3,500, £13,500, £27,000

Swap or no swap? No swap

Deal or No Deal? Deal!

Jason takes home £27,000

7

Contestants describing themselves as either 'realists' or 'both optimistic and pessimistic' have been the most successful winners

41

CONTESTANT

Name Helen Beer
Broadcast 16th December 2005

THE GAME

Starting box No 5, containing £20,000

Banker offers £800, £200, £1,500, £1,000, £2,000, £13,000

Swap or no swap? No swap

Deal or No Deal? Deal!

Helen takes home £13,000

DID YOU KNOW?

More contestants were born under the star sign Taurus than any other sign

42

CONTESTANT
Name Jeff Smith
Broadcast 17th December 2005

THE GAME
Starting box No 17, containing £5
Banker offers £2,100, £5,600, £1,600, £8,200, £12,400,
Swap or no swap? No swap
Deal or No Deal? Deal!

Jeff takes home £12,400

43

CONTESTANT
Name Karen Docherty
Broadcast 19th December 2005

THE GAME
Starting box No 15, containing £15,000
Banker offers £2,700, £900, £6,600, £17,000
Swap or no swap? No swap
Deal or No Deal? Deal!

Karen takes home £17,000

44

CONTESTANT
Name Mary-Ann Thorpe
Broadcast 20th December 2005

THE GAME
Starting box No 10, containing £50
Banker offers £2,000, £5,300, £14,000, £18,000
Swap or no swap? No swap
Deal or No Deal? Deal!

Mary Ann takes home £18,000

CONTESTANT

Name Christopher Jones

Broadcast 21st December 2005

THE GAME

Starting box No 2, containing £3,000

Banker offers £8,500, £2,700, £6,200, £24,000

Swap or no swap? No swap

Deal or No Deal? Deal!

45

Christopher takes home £24,000

46

Lucky Leo Lee Hartland beat The Banker and took home £50,000! Read his story overleaf.

CONTESTANT

Name Simon Cowley

Broadcast 23rd December 2005

THE GAME

Starting box No 7, containing £250

Banker offers £2,200, £4,700, £3,000, £13,000, £4,000, £400

Swap or no swap? No swap

Deal or No Deal? No deal

47

Simon takes home £250

CONTESTANT

Name Angela Sliman

Broadcast 26th December 2005

THE GAME

Starting box No 3, containing £750

Banker offers £7,500, £15,000, £22,700, £9,000, £18,200, £21,000

Swap or no swap? No swap

Deal or No Deal? Deal!

48

Angela takes home £21,000

CONTESTANT

Name Andy Bassett
Broadcast 27th December 2005

THE GAME

Starting box No 20, containing £500
Banker offers £1,800, £600, £7,000, £4,200, £13,000
Swap or no swap? No swap
Deal or No Deal? Deal!

Andy takes home £13,000

49

CONTESTANT

Name Michael Collins
Broadcast 28th December 2005

THE GAME

Starting box No 20, containing £750
Banker offers £8,100, £11,200, £3,700, £8,100, £18,000
Swap or no swap? No swap
Deal or No Deal? Deal!

Michael takes home £18,000

50

CONTESTANT

Name Louise Aspee
Broadcast 29th December 2005

THE GAME

Starting box No 14, containing 50p
Banker offers £500, £1,000, £1,900, £7,300, £9,000
Swap or no swap? No swap
Deal or No Deal? Deal!

Louise takes home £9,000

51

Contestants who wear glasses are bigger winners than those who don't

THE WALK OF WEALTH

PERSONAL FILE

Name
Lee Hartland

Broadcast
22nd December 2005

Occupation
Runs diamond drilling company

Star sign
Leo

Eye colour
Blue

Favourite number
1

Crisp flavour
Chicken

Favourite tipple
Lager

BANKER'S VERDICT

'Many players who are a powerful presence in the wings are not able to bring their courage and insight to the chair. Lee Hartland was not such a player. Formidable.'

BEFORE THE SHOW

'I'd never done anything like this before but I applied in the spirit of adventure, really. I don't take daily risks or gamble, but when I do go for it, it's a big, calculated, risk – like leaving work to set up my own company 15 years ago. On the show, I needed to come away with at least £2,000 to not make a loss, as I'd be missing out on a couple of weeks' work. The contestant friendship and team spirit was really strong, everyone wanted everyone else to do the best they possibly could. Then after the filming, when you got back to the hotel you had to pack a few pints in and wind down after the emotional day's games, to take away some of the pressure.'

THE GAME

'I've no particular lucky number, I haven't even got a house number – it's a name and my birthday's after the 22nd! So I just chose people if they caught my eye for any reason.

'I was nervous and I had a pretty terrible start, but I wasn't going to deal early – you're only up once and it's a now-or-never situation. I still had £75,000 and £250,000 on the board when The Banker made the £50,000 offer and I knew there and then I'd take it. I tried not to show it on my face, but I thought I'd be offered nearer £35,000 – certainly not as much as this!

'What was nice was that my show was on Noel Edmonds' birthday, so he was wearing a tuxedo and they brought out a cake at the end.'

Starting box
No 16, containing
£75,000

Blues cruise 4

Red run 4

Banker offers
£6,000, £3,000,
£12,000, £17,800,
£50,000

Swap or no swap?
No swap

Deal or No Deal?
Deal!

DEAL £50,000

Lee takes home £50,000

NOEL'S VERDICT
'I was concerned that the quiet Welshman had made a rod for his back by giving others such valuable advice. The Banker dislikes anyone who costs him money. However, Lee proved his worth as a businessman to play a business-like game and win a well-deserved £50,000.'

BACK TO REAL LIFE
What's the first thing you did when you got home?
'I phoned my parents then went out and celebrated with some other winners and had a Chinese. Thing is, it doesn't really hit you till the next day.'

What did you do with the money?
'We'd had our eye on buying a property in Spain for some years and now this gave us enough for a deposit. We've got the house now and it's become almost a hobby and recreation for us – and we named it "Casa Dond" in honour of the show!'

Was the show life-changing?
'I'm fundamentally the same person but the amount of money has helped me make some changes to life, or at least brought those things forward, like the house. It also opened my eyes to just how well, and how quickly, a bunch of really different people get on when they're thrown together like this.'

Any advice?
'Just enjoy it. Don't think about it too much and take it for what it is.'

52

CONTESTANT

Name Maxwell Freeman

Broadcast 30th December 2005

THE GAME

Starting box No 12, containing £10

Banker offers £1,400, £3,000, £6,000, £17,000, £30,000

Swap or no swap? No swap

Deal or No Deal? Deal!

Maxwell takes home £30,000

53

CONTESTANT

Name Irene Christie

Broadcast 2nd January 2006

THE GAME

Starting box No 17, containing £250

Banker offers £1,700, £2,400, £2,000, £4,700, £800, £100

Swap or no swap? Swapped to Box 15, containing £5

Deal or No Deal? No deal

Irene takes home £5

54

Unlucky **Nick Bain** got offered £9,000 but turned it down to become the first member of the exclusive 1p Club! Read his story overleaf.

55

CONTESTANT

Name Jenni Brooks

Broadcast 4th January 2006

THE GAME

Starting box No 17, containing £50,000

Banker offers £3,400, £8,100, £26,000

Swap or no swap? No swap

Deal or No Deal? Deal!

Jenni takes home £26,000

DID YOU KNOW?

Fewer contestants were born under the star sign Scorpio than any other sign

56

CONTESTANT
Name Dave Woollin
Broadcast 5th January 2006

THE GAME
Starting box No 21, containing 10p
Banker offers £4,321, £9,000, £6,000, £12,000, £20,000
Swap or no swap? No swap
Deal or No Deal? Deal!

Dave takes home £20,000

57

CONTESTANT
Name Pat Stenning-Hawkes
Broadcast 6th January 2006

THE GAME
Starting box No 21, containing £100
Banker offers £2,200, £2,200, £8,400, £6,000, £2,300, £1,000
Swap or no swap? Swapped to Box 5, containing £3,000
Deal or No Deal? No deal

Pat takes home £3,000

58

CONTESTANT
Name Gavin Gallagher
Broadcast 7th January 2006

THE GAME
Starting box No 11, containing £5
Banker offers £3,600, £4,000, £9,000, £6,000, £10,000
Swap or no swap? No swap
Deal or No Deal? Deal!

Gavin takes home £10,000

THE 1p CLUB

PERSONAL FILE

Name
Nick Bain

Broadcast
3rd January 2006

Occupation
Mortgage sales support

Star sign
Scorpio

Eye colour
Hazel

Favourite number
7

Crisp flavour
Marmite

Favourite tipple
Rum and coke

BANKER'S VERDICT

'Handsome. Charming. Intelligent. And excellent value. Nick is the founder of my favourite club. I have his photograph on my office wall to this very day.'

BEFORE THE SHOW

'I saw the trailer for the show and the lure was the money. I wanted to win enough to get me and my wife Stacy out of our money troubles, so we could spend our wages and get a bit more settled instead of paying off loans. Being in that hotel was the best two-and-a-half weeks I've ever had. Everyone wanted everyone else to do well, we went out for a few drinks every night, and down to the Chinese restaurant for meals. You couldn't have asked for a better set of people.

'I did 22 shows before I was on. Most days, I'd wear lemon or yellow, and Noel and I had a great banter about my bright shirts and tank tops. One day I was in a plain blue T-shirt, not the greatest of tops to go on telly, to be honest, and they picked me! I was so shocked I was shaking like a leaf.'

THE GAME

'To start with, the game went really well. I didn't have a game plan, I was just picking boxes randomly. I thought about keeping back 18 and 11, because my birthday is on the 18th November. I still think about that now, because they contained the £100,000 and £75,000! Generally I'm not an unlucky person, but then I took out eight reds in a row. Eight! It was unbelievable. I was laughing because the game couldn't get any worse, but inside I was dying.

'In the end it was down to all blues, and I thought, why not see if I can win the penny. I'll be the first person to do it, and although it's not the greatest achievement, it is an achievement of sorts. I did a swap, and got it! After the show, I had to ring up Stacy and tell her the bad news. I'm a bit of a practical joker and she genuinely thought I was having her on – I had to get Michelle the Care AP to explain it was true. That night in Dave's room, 10 of us drank wine and had a cry. It was really emotional.'

Starting box
No 5, containing £100

Blues cruise 4

Red run 8

Banker offers
£1,300, £900, £9,000, £4,500, £3,000, £30

Swap or no swap?
Swapped to box 3, containing 1p

Deal or No Deal?
No deal

Nick takes home 1p

NOEL'S VERDICT

'Nick was the very first member of the 1p club – a label that everyone dreaded. He brilliantly concealed his abject horror and disappointment at what was happening. This was a milestone in Deal or No Deal history, but Nick managed somehow to carry it off with good grace.'

BACK TO REAL LIFE

What's the first thing you did when you got home?
'My wife Stacy gave me a big cuddle. Then I went to bed for two days feeling sorry for myself!'

What did you do with the money?
'The cheque had a note on it saying I'd joined an exclusive club, and was signed by Noel. We're going to frame it and put it in the spare room as memorabilia of the show.'

Was the show life-changing?
'No. Even though I was devastated it didn't change me at all. I've since had a bit of infamy with people recognising me, and it might have helped me get a new job as a recruitment executive. But I'm still as positive as ever. That day wasn't my day, but I know my day will come.'

Any advice?
'Go with what you feel, and don't listen to anyone's advice.'

59

CONTESTANT

Name Jenna Wall
Broadcast 9th January 2006

THE GAME

Starting box No 9, containing £5,000
Banker offers £2,500, £900, £3,600, £1,300, £4,000, £1,500
Swap or no swap? No swap
Deal or No Deal? No deal

Jenna takes home £5,000

60

CONTESTANT

Name Lynsey Dowle
Broadcast 10th January 2006

THE GAME

Starting box No 1, containing £5
Banker offers £5,000, £3,100, £6,700, £1,500, £8,600
Swap or no swap? No swap
Deal or No Deal? Deal!

Lynsey takes home £8,600

18

Contestants who don't own pets have been bigger money winners on average than those who own pets

61

CONTESTANT

Name Michael Daly
Broadcast 11th January 2006

THE GAME

Starting box No 1, containing 10p
Banker offers £2,300, £1,900, £8,900, £9,900
Swap or no swap? No swap
Deal or No Deal? Deal!

Michael takes home £9,900

62

CONTESTANT
Name Robbie Pollard
Broadcast 12th January 2006

THE GAME
Starting box No 19, containing £5,00
Banker offers £7,100, £14,900, £16,000, £12,000, £5,500
Swap or no swap? No swap
Deal or No Deal? Deal!

Robbie takes home £5,500

63

CONTESTANT
Name Arlette Rose
Broadcast 13th January 2006

THE GAME
Starting box No 9, containing 10p
Banker offers £2,400, £6,800, £13,000, £21,000
Swap or no swap? No swap
Deal or No Deal? Deal!

Arlette takes home £21,000

64

CONTESTANT
Name Alan Bradfield
Broadcast 14th January 2006

THE GAME
Starting box No 21, containing £5,000
Banker offers £220, £2,200, £2,500, £400, £1,000
Swap or no swap? No swap
Deal or No Deal? Deal!

Alan takes home £1,000

65

CONTESTANT
Name Vaughan Evans
Broadcast 16th January 2006

THE GAME
Starting box No 5, containing 10p
Banker offers £3,300, £5,900, £8,000, £18,000, £4,900
Swap or no swap? No swap
Deal or No Deal? Deal!

Vaughan takes home £4,900

PERSONAL FILE

Name Gill Lee-Ireland
Broadcast 17th January 2006
Occupation Training consultant
Star sign Taurus
Eye colour Brown
Favourite number 8
Crisp flavour Cheese and onion
Favourite tipple Spritzer

66

" I was on maternity leave with five-month-old Holly, so had time on my hands and thought why not have a go? I spent two weeks in Bristol filming 30 shows – the first week my husband Craig and Holly were in the hotel with me, but the second week they went home to Fife, and I missed them terribly. Contestants who'd arrived after me had been and gone, and I thought there wasn't a chance I'd get on before filming stopped for Christmas. It was the last show when my name was called – I was genuinely shocked. But then it's just you and Noel and those 22 boxes, and that's all you focus on. "

THE GAME

" Noel was so warm and funny. I'm just short of 5ft 2in, and every time the camera panned on me when I was holding a box, I'd go on tiptoes to try and look taller. He started taking the mickey out of me, saying I was compact, and the best things come in small packages. A bit like him! I didn't have a plan – just picked some memorable numbers from my family's birthdays. I was convinced I had £75,000 in my box, and when I got offered £11,000, it was on the tip of my tongue to say no. I'm glad I didn't... The money came in very handy – we had a lovely Christmas, put a deposit down on an Audi A4, and had two big weddings abroad. "

Starting box No 18, containing £250
Blues cruise 3
Red run 4
Banker offers £2,800, £8,100, £1,600, £7,200, £11,000
Swap or no swap? No swap
Deal or No Deal? Deal!

Gill takes home £11,000

67

CONTESTANT

Name Terry Rayner

Broadcast 18th January 2006

THE GAME

Starting box No 7, containing 10p

Banker offers £3,000, £3,000, £6,000, £4,500, £24,500

Swap or no swap? No swap

Deal or No Deal? Deal!

Terry takes home £24,500

68

CONTESTANT

Name Julie Walton

Broadcast 19th January 2006

THE GAME

Starting box No 11, containing 1p

Banker offers £1,300, £800, £3,200, £7,100, £33,000

Swap or no swap? No swap

Deal or No Deal? Deal!

Julie takes home £33,000

DID YOU KNOW?

3.5% of contestants have had £250,000 in their box

69

CONTESTANT

Name Miguel Moreno-Melgan

Broadcast 20th January 2006

THE GAME

Starting box No 7, containing £5,000

Banker offers £4,000, £6,800, £10,000, £21,000

Swap or no swap? No swap

Deal or No Deal? Deal!

Miguel takes home £21,000

70

CONTESTANT

Name Garvan Tohill
Broadcast 21st January 2006

THE GAME

Starting box No 4, containing £5,000
Banker offers £700, £4,000, £6,000, £14,500, £13,000, £1,500
Swap or no swap? No swap
Deal or No Deal? No deal

Garvan takes home £5,000

71

CONTESTANT

Name Ann Harding
Broadcast 23rd January 2006

THE GAME

Starting box No 6, containing 50p
Banker offers £7,000, £2,000, £700, £11,700, £3,000, £100
Swap or no swap? Swapped to Box 16, containg £250
Deal or No Deal? No deal

Ann takes home £250

72

CONTESTANT

Name Gerald Burton
Broadcast 24th January 2006

THE GAME

Starting box No 1, containing £10
Banker offers £5,800, £3,100, £1,500, £11,700
Swap or no swap? No swap
Deal or No Deal? Deal!

Gerald takes home £11,700

73

CONTESTANT

Name Liz Stokes
Broadcast 25th January 2006

THE GAME

Starting box No 16, containing £35,000
Banker offers £1,100, £300, £5,300, £8,100, £17,000
Swap or no swap? No swap
Deal or No Deal? Deal!

Liz takes home £17,000

74

CONTESTANT

Name Andrew Weir
Broadcast 26th January 2006

THE GAME

Starting box No 13, containing £10
Banker offers £2,200, £600, £14,000
Swap or no swap? No swap
Deal or No Deal? Deal!

Andrew takes home £14,000

75

CONTESTANT

Name Jessica Ezeogu
Broadcast 27th January 2006

THE GAME

Starting box No 15, containing £35,000
Banker offers £3,700, £2,000, £4,000, £12,500, £41,000
Swap or no swap? No swap
Deal or No Deal? Deal!

Jessica takes home £41,000

Only 9% of contestants have been left-handed

76

CONTESTANT
Name Rosemarie Apps
Broadcast 28th January 2006

THE GAME
Starting box No 7, containing £10,000

Banker offers £9,000, £15,000, £30,000, £8,000, £6,000, £4,000

Swap or no swap? No swap

Deal or No Deal? Deal!

Rosemarie takes home £4,000

77

CONTESTANT
Name Charles Ladlow
Broadcast 30th January 2006

THE GAME
Starting box No 21, containing £100,000

Banker offers £4,000, £10,000, £7,000, £12,000

Swap or no swap? No swap

Deal or No Deal? Deal!

Charles takes home £12,000

78

CONTESTANT
Name Mumtaz Begum Khan
Broadcast 31st January 2006

THE GAME
Starting box No 18, containing 50p

Banker offers £3,200, £3,200, £1,600, £9,600, £24,000

Swap or no swap? No swap

Deal or No Deal? Deal!

Mumtaz takes home £24,000

79

CONTESTANT

Name Gerry Reynolds
Broadcast 1st February 2006

THE GAME

Starting box No 21, containing 10p
Banker offers £500, £750, £200, £5,000, £80, £20
Swap or no swap? No swap
Deal or No Deal? Deal!

Gerry takes home £20

80

CONTESTANT

Name Vanessa Buck
Broadcast 2nd February 2006

THE GAME

Starting box No 3, containing £20,000
Banker offers £6,200, £2,000, £300, £4,400, £2,200, £5,500
Swap or no swap? No swap
Deal or No Deal? No deal

Vanessa takes home £20,000

81

CONTESTANT

Name Jim Percival
Broadcast 3rd February 2006

THE GAME

Starting box No 15, containing 10p
Banker offers £4,200, £10,500, £6,000, £4,000, £17,000
Swap or no swap? No swap
Deal or No Deal? Deal!

Jim takes home £17,000

Contestants with tattoos have won 36% more money on average than those who don't have tattoos

82

CONTESTANT

Name Aileen Boag
Broadcast 4th February 2006

THE GAME

Starting box No 1, containing £100
Banker offers £2,800, £1,400, £800, £11,000, £8,000
Swap or no swap? No swap
Deal or No Deal? Deal!

Aileen takes home £8,000

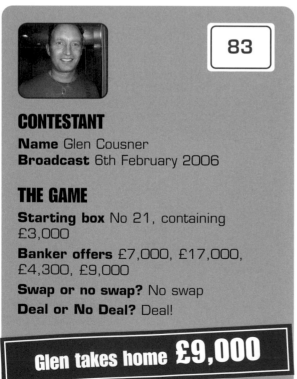

83

CONTESTANT

Name Glen Cousner
Broadcast 6th February 2006

THE GAME

Starting box No 21, containing £3,000
Banker offers £7,000, £17,000, £4,300, £9,000
Swap or no swap? No swap
Deal or No Deal? Deal!

Glen takes home £9,000

DID YOU KNOW?

85% of contestants describe themselves as optimists

PERSONAL FILE

84

Name John Magill
Broadcast 7th February 2006
Occupation Retired postman
Star sign Virgo
Eye colour Brown
Favourite number 14
Crisp flavour Ready salted
Favourite tipple Bacardi and coke

"Two years before the show I'd had a quadruple heart bypass, followed by stomach surgery, and had stitches all the way down from my throat to my tummy. I'm usually a very jolly person, but I was feeling a bit depressed and when I saw the ad to take part in the show, I thought it would be something to get me back on my feet and interested in life again. And it worked. I was in the hotel for 32 shows and got close to so many lovely people. It cheered me up no end."

THE GAME

"I decided to knock out the men first in descending order by age – except for Box 14, my lucky number. Then I'd start on the women. It worked well until I lost the £250,000 box, because at my advanced age all young people look the same, couldn't tell which one of two girls should go first – and I picked the wrong one! The banker knew my lucky number and when he offered me £14,000 (after I'd turned down £28,000 - argh!), I took it. It was lovely to win the money – I gave £10,000 to my daughter to pay off her university overdraft, and my wife Margaret and I went on a great holiday in Tenerife."

Starting box No 6, containing £1
Blues cruise 2
Red run 2
Banker offers £3,600, £8,200, £13,013, £6,660, £28,000, £14,000
Swap or no swap? No swap
Deal or No Deal? Deal!

John takes home £14,000

85

CONTESTANT
Name Linda Gibson
Broadcast 8th February 2006

THE GAME
Starting box No 3, containing £3,000
Banker offers £4,000, £9,200, £13,800, £6,000, £16,000
Swap or no swap? No swap
Deal or No Deal? Deal!

Linda takes home £16,000

Brown-eyed contestants win more on average than blue-eyed contestants

86

Green-eyed Scorpio **Brenda Currie** had the audience on her side when she took on The Banker to win a fantastic £57,000. Read her story overleaf.

87

CONTESTANT
Name Peter Haslam
Broadcast 10th February 2006

THE GAME
Starting box No 20, containing £5
Banker offers £8,000, £5,000, £3,000, £3,500
Swap or no swap? No swap
Deal or No Deal? Deal!

Peter takes home £3,500

PERSONAL FILE

88

Name Daz Stokes
Broadcast 11th February 2006
Occupation Entertainment advisor
Star sign Pisces
Eye colour Green
Favourite number 16
Crisp flavour Cheese and onion
Favourite tipple Baileys

"A year ago, the roof was leaking, we had no cooker and no Christmas dinner, and I remember watching Deal or No Deal on the TV and thinking, this is a chance to improve my life and change things for the better. I'm a down-to-earth family guy and we'd had a bad time since my father's death, so I wanted to give my mum some money and help her out."

THE GAME

"I was awash with emotion sitting in that chair. I went for people's faces, jolly people I connected with. Noel and I clicked really well – we both had loud shirts on, and there was a bit of banter about that. When The Banker offered me £45,000, I had a gut feeling it was the right time to go. The 1p was still on the board and I was thinking I can't blow this, my mum needs a new front door! Winning felt like a dream – I've had 21 jobs in 20 years and could never hope to earn that kind of money. We've had a new porch and double glazing put in, been to Corfu and Barcelona, and I've just bought a 50-in plasma telly, my pride and joy. I've given up my job, joined a talent agency in London, and my dream is to get a job as a presenter on a shopping channel. Going on Deal or No Deal turned my life around and got me out of a deep, dark hole. It's fantastic, I'm still on a high."

Starting box No 10, containing £250,000
Blues cruise 5
Red run 6
Banker offers £6,900, £2,000, £5,000, £19,000, £45,000
Swap or no swap? No swap
Deal or No Deal? Deal!

Daz takes home £45,000

THE WALK OF WEALTH

PERSONAL FILE

Name
Brenda Currie

Broadcast
9th February 2006

Occupation
Medical receptionist

Star sign
Scorpio

Eye colour
Green

Favourite number
5

Crisp flavour
Ready salted

Favourite tipple
Vodka and lemonade

BANKER'S VERDICT

'Mathematically, a wildly improbable game. I began to worry Brenda had mental powers which enabled her to see through the very fabric of the boxes. To lose the £57K was a relief in the end; I thought she was headed for the big one.'

BEFORE THE SHOW

'It was very out of character for me to go on a TV quiz show, but it was meant to be. Something guided me – fate if you will. Beforehand I thought, "£5,000 would be nice, £10,000 would be great, and anything above that – pull me down from the chandeliers!" But mostly I just wanted to be able not to worry so much about money and have a bit of freedom with it.

'The other contestants were brilliant, everyone looks out for each other. They all called me "Second Mam", and I got a certificate presented to me – The Mrs Doubtfire Award for everyone's favourite mother! Being called up was terrifying. I was paralysed with nerves and went into shock. You can't be prepared for it.'

THE GAME

'I was shaking as I was miked up. The crew member said, "You're very quiet, Brenda", and it wasn't like me at all. He then said, "Just go on and be yourself", so that's what I did. I had a very lucky game really. The thing I was most nervous about was talking to Noel Edmonds! The atmosphere was quite electric – the audience were chanting "Bren-da, Bren-da!" – really supportive. At the point of the £57,000 offer, I could have held on but I spoke to The Banker myself and he said, "Take the money, Brenda", and I did. After that, when you have to play on regardless, he offered me £84,000 and I thought, "I'll kill him!"'

DEAL £57,000

Starting box
No 11, containing
£50,000

Blues cruise 5

Red run 5

Banker offers
£7,500, £15,000,
£31,000, £57,000

Swap or no swap?
No swap

Deal or No Deal?
Deal!

Brenda takes home £57,000

NOEL'S VERDICT
'Brenda was undoubtedly one of our most nervous players initially, but she managed to regain control. She had reached a key moment when she spoke to The Banker and it was such a shame that she fell for his charms!'

BACK TO REAL LIFE

What's the first thing you did when you got home?
'I went to my local pub where there was a bit of a do on. It wasn't for me, but it still felt celebratory. After the programme came out, I got a standing ovation when I walked into the same local! I think people are pleased to see someone like me – a council estate woman who brought her two children up as a single mother – doing well for themselves.'

What did you do with the money?
'I've had a couple of foreign holidays and weekends away, but the main things were buying a caravan near where my twin brother has one in Northumberland, and getting the house totally redecorated and the garden landscaped. People who come to my house say it looks like I had one of those home makeover shows on it!'

Was the show life-changing?
'When a bill comes through the door, or I fancy a dinner out, I don't have to worry "Can I afford it?" My quality of life has greatly improved.

Any advice?
'You can't really give advice – everyone's game is so different.'

89

CONTESTANT
Name Chris Robbins
Broadcast 13th February 2006

THE GAME
Starting box No 1, containing £5
Banker offers £2,200, £4,400, £800, £1,500
Swap or no swap? No swap
Deal or No Deal? Deal!

Chris takes home £1,500

90

CONTESTANT
Name Helen Richards-Decrew
Broadcast 14th February 2006

THE GAME
Starting box No 9, containing £3,000
Banker offers £2,800, £4,100, £2,000, £4,800
Swap or no swap? No swap
Deal or No Deal? Deal!

Helen takes home £4,800

91

CONTESTANT
Name Benita Hobbs
Broadcast 15th February 2006

THE GAME
Starting box No 1, containing 10p
Banker offers £5,200, £1,800, £3,500, £9,000, £27,000
Swap or no swap? No swap
Deal or No Deal? Deal!

Benita takes home £27,000

DID YOU KNOW?

Of those contestants who've had **£250,000** in their box, their average eventual winnings were **£39,125**

92

CONTESTANT
Name Russell Cook
Broadcast 16th February 2006

THE GAME
Starting box No 13, containing £500
Banker offers £1,000, £2,000, £7,500, £21,000
Swap or no swap? No swap
Deal or No Deal? Deal!

Russell takes home £21,000

93

CONTESTANT
Name Paula Richards
Broadcast 17th February 2006

THE GAME
Starting box No 4, containing £500
Banker offers £2,700, £3,000, £5,000, £16,400
Swap or no swap? No swap
Deal or No Deal? Deal!

Paula takes home £16,400

94

CONTESTANT
Name John Gilbert
Broadcast 18th February 2006

THE GAME
Starting box No 21, containing £250
Banker offers £8, £5,100, £9,500, £5,700, £25,000, £90
Swap or no swap? Swapped to Box 7, containing £10
Deal or No Deal? No deal

John takes home £10

95

CONTESTANT
Name Finlay McLoughlin
Broadcast 20th February 2006

THE GAME
Starting box No 1, containing £20,000
Banker offers £900, £2,300, £11,000, £44,000, £3,000, £15,000
Swap or no swap? Swapped to Box 19, containing £10,000
Deal or No Deal? No deal

Finlay takes home £10,000

96

CONTESTANT
Name Donna Cromb
Broadcast 21st February 2006

THE GAME
Starting box No 3, containing £10,000
Banker offers £4,300, £9,100, £12,000, £8,000, £10,100
Swap or no swap? No swap
Deal or No Deal? Deal!

Donna takes home £10,100

97

CONTESTANT
Name Paul Lawrinson
Broadcast 22nd February 2006

THE GAME
Starting box No 2, containing £1
Banker offers £5,500, £13,000, £19,400, £5,400, £24,000
Swap or no swap? No swap
Deal or No Deal? Deal!

Paul takes home £24,000

Contestants who went to university have won 9% more on average than those who didn't

98

CONTESTANT

Name Okiem Warmann
Broadcast 23rd February 2006

THE GAME

Starting box No 10, containing £50
Banker offers £8,100, £1,900, £4,900, £6,500, £2,500, £17,000
Swap or no swap? No swap
Deal or No Deal? Deal!

Okiern takes home £17,000

99

CONTESTANT

Name Beryl Urquhart
Broadcast 24th February 2006

THE GAME

Starting box No 6, containing £15,000
Banker offers £2,800, £1,400, £3,100
Swap or no swap? No swap
Deal or No Deal? Deal!

Beryl takes home £3,100

100

CONTESTANT

Name Anna Scott
Broadcast 25th February 2006

THE GAME

Starting box No 11, containing £250,000
Banker offers £7,300, £11,200, £3,700, £13,000, £43,000
Swap or no swap? No swap
Deal or No Deal? Deal!

Anna takes home £43,000

101

CONTESTANT

Name Gary Conrad
Broadcast 27th February 2006

THE GAME

Starting box No 2, containing £10,000
Banker offers £5,500, £11,000, £4,000, £1,300, £11,050, £11,900
Swap or no swap? Swapped to Box 8, containing £15,000
Deal or No Deal? No deal

Gary takes home £15,000

102

CONTESTANT

Name Tracey Nicholls
Broadcast 28th February 2006

THE GAME

Starting box No 9, containing £250
Banker offers £1,400, £700, £1,800, £3,600, £1,500, £2,900
Swap or no swap? No swap
Deal or No Deal? Deal!

Tracey takes home £2,900

103

Trevor Bruce went for the big one but it wasn't to be his lucky day. He took home a cheque for 1p, entering the portals of the exclusive 1p Club! Read his story overleaf.

104

CONTESTANT

Name Michael Spargo
Broadcast 2nd March 2006

THE GAME

Starting box No 5, containing £1
Banker offers £5,200, £2,000, £1,200, £3,200, £1,200, £30
Swap or no swap? No swap
Deal or No Deal? No deal

Michael takes home £1

105

CONTESTANT

Name Norma Wiles
Broadcast 3rd March 2006

THE GAME

Starting box No 5, containing £15,000
Banker offers £1,300, £2,200, £8,500, £13,000, £26,000
Swap or no swap? No swap
Deal or No Deal? Deal!

Norma takes home £26,000

PERSONAL FILE

106

Name Sam Simmons
Broadcast 4th March 2006
Occupation Model
Star sign Capricorn
Eye colour Brown
Favourite number 21
Crisp flavour Marmite
Favourite tipple Gin and tonic

"I wanted to leave my job but I had a lot of debt and couldn't go unless I got made redundant – or won a game show. So when I saw the ad saying: "Do you want to win a life-changing sum of money?", I thought, yes please. I'm a really competitive person and I wanted to play the best game I possibly could. I did 26 shows, and on the day the atmosphere was electric - very few things in life give you that extreme of emotion. The whole experience made me believe there is something more out there and if you really believe in yourself you can make anything happen."

THE GAME

"It gave me such a buzz to beat The Banker. I turned down £33,000 but then I knocked the big one out and the Banker's offer dropped to £12,000. I kept playing until we were down to £15,000 and £75,000. For some reason I was convinced I had £75,000 in my box. The banker offered £41,000 and I just broke down in tears. I couldn't decide whether to take the deal or hang out for the bigger sum. My heart was saying go for it, but my head was saying be sensible. I was in complete turmoil. Everyone in the audience was chanting and then through it all I heard my dad's voice saying, "Deal", and that swung it. Thank heavens, because I had the £15,000 in my box"

Starting box No 20, containing £15,000
Blues cruise 3
Red run 3
Banker offers £4,900, £12,400, £21,000, £33,000, £12,000, £41,000
Swap or no swap? No swap
Deal or No Deal? Deal!

Sam takes home £41,000

THE 1p CLUB

PERSONAL FILE

Name
Trevor Bruce

Broadcast
1st March 2006

Occupation
Retired

Star sign
Libra

Eye colour
Grey

Favourite number
5

Crisp flavour
Salt and vinegar

Favourite tipple
Whisky

BANKER'S VERDICT

'Unbelievably unlucky. But for his final choice, he might have walked away with over £50,000 – maybe more. A gentleman who I expect brought a real air of class to that rather grubby little phone box.'

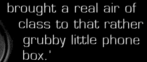

BEFORE THE SHOW

'I applied when the show first started. I thought, "You don't need any special talent to do that... just be a gambler." I had a particular goal in mind: I wanted £10,000 for a business-class trip to Australia to see my brother. I'd always put off going because I couldn't face another long-haul journey in economy, but then I dreamt my brother had died. My wife said, "Why don't you just go out there?"

'When it's your turn to go up, you're in shock – you're worried about saying and doing the wrong thing. Basically, you just hope you come across with a bit of dignity! The days were enjoyable but hard work – fun but stressful, if that makes any sense. There are several shows to film a day, wardrobe, make-up, meals... And your mind never rests because you are rooting so hard for the other contestants too.'

THE GAME

'I was very nervous to begin with, so Noel played a word-association game to make me laugh and calm me down. He asked for my first reaction to the word "Viagra". "Wonderful," I said. "Oh, and by the way, Noel, the 72-hour ones are much better than the 12-hour!" which had the team and audience in stitches.

'The game plan nearly worked, if I can say such a thing. I'd gone with family birth dates and I still had my £250,000 box unopened down to the last three, but The Banker never offered me more than £9,900. I think he had it in for me, definitely. If I'd have been younger and a woman, I bet he'd have stumped up £20,000 or even £30,000! I tried to negotiate with him to settle at £30,000, but he said "No deal". At this point, I was feeling very confident as I felt certain the £250,000 box was in front of me. Well, it wasn't!

'Some friends – female ones from my old work place – said they burst into tears when it was broadcast and I ended up with just 1p. That was really very sweet.'

Starting box
No 14, containing 1p

Blues cruise 3

Red run 5

Banker offers
£1,100, £7,500, £3,500, £9,900,
£9,900, £99

Swap or no swap?
No swap

Deal or No Deal?
No deal

Trevor takes home 1p

NOEL'S VERDICT

'Trevor had a cerebral approach to everybody's game which is why, game after game, the players would ask for his advice. It was just such a shame that his game played out in such a way that he was powerless to do anything to alter the outcome.'

BACK TO REAL LIFE

What's the first thing you did when you got home?
'Not much! But immediately after my 'win' or loss, should I say, one of the crew came for a walk round the grounds with me, then we watched the next show to take my mind off it.'

What did you do with the money?
'I've got it framed with a photo taken of me next to Noel. A lady viewer sent the show a cheque made out to "Trevor Deal or No Deal". She insisted on finding out my real surname and writing me another cheque! Now, why can't another thousand viewers do that!'

Was the show life-changing?
'Well, no. But me and the wife had a couple of week's stay in a hotel and were well fed out of it. A lot of my friends have come up and offered me a penny to "double your winnings", none of them knowing they're about the tenth person to do so. My golf buddies had some shirts made up with 'Deal or Noel Deal' and one for me with '1p Club'. Oh, and I've booked a flight out to Australia next year. So it's not all bad.'

Any advice?
'I don't think I can, can I!'

CONTESTANT

Name Lisa Haak

Broadcast 6th March 2006

THE GAME

Starting box No 1, containing £1

Banker offers £3,000, £1,200, £9,000, £20,000

Swap or no swap? No swap

Deal or No Deal? Deal!

107

Lisa takes home £20,000

Piscean lorry-driver **Germaine Williams** had the game of a lifetime to take home a fantastic £75,000 offer from The Banker! Read his story overleaf.

108

Box 2 is the luckiest box – £250,000 has appeared in it the most times

CONTESTANT

Name Candice Watt-Roy

Broadcast 8th March 2006

THE GAME

Starting box No 22, containing £500

Banker offers £4,000, £12,000, £21,000, £32,000, £19,000

Swap or no swap? No swap

Deal or No Deal? Deal!

109

Candice takes home £19,000

DID YOU KNOW?

Non-drinkers are bigger winners on average than drinkers

110

CONTESTANT
Name Paula Henry
Broadcast 9th March 2006

THE GAME
Starting box No 22, containing £10,000
Banker offers £1,800, £11,000, £4,000, £7,000, £10,022
Swap or no swap? No swap
Deal or No Deal? Deal!

Paula takes home £10,022

111

CONTESTANT
Name Patrick Kennedy
Broadcast 10th March 2006

THE GAME
Starting box No 12, containing £100,000
Banker offers £2,000, £9,000, £17,000, £15,000, £15,500
Swap or no swap? No swap
Deal or No Deal? Deal!

Patrick takes home £15,500

112

CONTESTANT
Name Marcus Neill
Broadcast 11th March 2006

THE GAME
Starting box No 14, containing £100
Banker offers £8,200, £16,500, £23,000, £31,000
Swap or no swap? No swap
Deal or No Deal? Deal!

Marcus takes home £31,000

THE WALK OF WEALTH

PERSONAL FILE

Name
Germaine Williams

Broadcast
7th March 2006

Occupation
Lorry driver

Star sign
Pisces

Eye colour
Brown

Favourite number
2

Pet owner
Yes

Favourite tipple
Alcohol…

BANKER'S VERDICT

'Popular players are my absolute favourites. When I snap them like dry twigs, a cloud of poisonous fear envelops the entire group. Germaine was just… the one that got away. With 75 grand. But I beat him, do you hear me?'

BEFORE THE SHOW

'I'm a night-shift worker and when I get home from work in the small hours, I sometimes sit in the garden and look at the stars… I wanted to win a life-changing sum – basically more than I could get a loan for! But really, around £15,000 would be enough to improve life, money-wise.

'The whole atmosphere at the hotel is like a fantastic cult. When I first got there I thought they were all nutters, hugging me, kissing me, never met me before and all a bit happy-clappy. After two days, I was just the same, if not worse! It's funny but even though you know it's logic that you'll go on at some point and you should be prepared, you're not. There's a massive build-up to this pinnacle and then you're petrified.'

DEAL £75,000

THE GAME

'Lots of people – complete strangers sometimes – tell me they thought it was the best game they'd ever seen. Poor Noel, I didn't give him much to work with because I was determined to keep a poker face. I was left with some decent reds and although I felt I knew I had the £250,000 in my box, it wasn't worth taking the risk in case it was the remaining blue – £1– and I couldn't go home with that. I was nervous but I didn't want to give The Banker anything to go on. I did feel a bit cheated that I accepted a lower amount than was in my box, even though I'd just won a small fortune! It took a couple of weeks to sink in.'

NOEL'S VERDICT

'What impressed me about Germaine's game was that he had an air of bravado, but at the crucial moment remembered where his priorities lay. I like family-orientated winners!'

Starting box
No 12, containing £250,000

Blues cruise 4

Red run 3

Banker offers
£2,700, £6,500, £16,500, £1,000, £28,000, £75,000

Swap or no swap?
No swap

Deal or No Deal?
Deal!

Germaine takes home **£75,000**

BACK TO REAL LIFE

What's the first thing you did when you got home?
'Went home, kissed the wife, hugged the kids, got drunk.'

What did you do with the money?
'We've bought a villa on the Aegean coast and that should pay for itself back, value-wise. We also threw a party in our local on the day showing my game on the big sports screen. It was like watching England in the World Cup in there – cheering, shouting, punching the air.'

Was the show life-changing?
'We, the whole family, owe a debt of gratitude to the team, the crew, to Noel. It's given us the kick up the backside we needed and changed our outlook on life. We're looking through new windows and opening other doors from now on.'

Any advice?
'If you get an offer, mentally go out and spend that amount. If you don't feel passionate for that thing, it might just be worth gambling for more, but if it gives you great pleasure then it's worth dealing.'

113

CONTESTANT

Name Sarah Harrison
Broadcast 13th March 2006

THE GAME

Starting box No 22, containing £1
Banker offers £6,000, £9,100, £4,000, £27,000
Swap or no swap? No swap
Deal or No Deal? Deal!

Sarah takes home £27,000

114

CONTESTANT

Name Flash Wilson
Broadcast 14th March 2006

THE GAME

Starting box No 1, containing £5,000
Banker offers £727, £3,025, £6,000
Swap or no swap? No swap
Deal or No Deal? Deal!

Flash takes home £6,000

Non-drivers have won more on average than drivers

115

CONTESTANT

Name David Williams
Broadcast 15th March 2006

THE GAME

Starting box No 3, containing £10,000
Banker offers £6,000, £3,800, £7,500, £17,000, £15,000, £30,000
Swap or no swap? No swap
Deal or No Deal? Deal!

David takes home £30,000

117

CONTESTANT

Name James McEvaddy
Broadcast 17th March 2006

THE GAME

Starting box No 21, containing £100,000

Banker offers £7,000, £14,000, £21,000, £9,000, £32,000

Swap or no swap? No swap

Deal or No Deal? Deal!

James takes home £32,000

116

Lucky Libran **Sajela Sarfraz** had box number 11 containing the £50,000 she eventually took home. Read her amazing story overleaf.

118

CONTESTANT

Name Jim Robertson
Broadcast 18th March 2006

THE GAME

Starting box No 16, containing £3,000

Banker offers £1,900, £6,000, £18,000, £2,800, £1,700, £1,100

Swap or no swap? Swapped to Box 18, containing £500

Deal or No Deal? No deal

Jim takes home £500

119

CONTESTANT

Name Barbara Norton
Broadcast 20th March 2006

THE GAME

Starting box No 8, containing £1

Banker offers £4,500, £9,000, £2,500, £11,500, £8,500, £3

Swap or no swap? No swap

Deal or No Deal? No deal

Barbara takes home £1

THE WALK OF WEALTH

PERSONAL FILE

Name
Sajela Sarfraz

Broadcast
16th March 2006

Occupation
Administration supervisor

Star sign
Libra

Eye colour
Brown

Favourite number
7

Crisp flavour
Chicken

Favourite tipple
Water

BANKER'S VERDICT

'Beautiful, beautiful Sajela; I know we could have had something special… if you hadn't nabbed all my cash. After her astonishingly courageous big win, Sajela sent me a card which read "When I count my blessings, I will count you 50,000 times." I burnt it.'

BEFORE THE SHOW

'I was on maternity leave and my husband wasn't working. We'd bought a house a year before, and were really struggling. I thought, what better way to get a few thousand pounds? I didn't have high hopes because I've never been a lucky person or won anything before, not even a teddy bear in a raffle. I thought this was a good opportunity but I wouldn't get my hopes up – £3,000 would be fine.

'Being at the hotel was brilliant, like joining a new family. Intense bonding like that can only happen in situations where you're all aiming for the same goal, and everyone wanted to boost everyone else's confidence and raise the morale of the group higher. In the breaks, Germaine and Candice and I used to do this 80s' dance routine. Germaine would do a wiggle, and there'd be lots of banter between the east and west side. I'm normally a quiet person and don't mind taking a back seat, but when I was the centre of attention, I knew I'd be able to handle the pressure. In fact I think I shocked a lot of my family, who hadn't seen me be that confident before.'

THE GAME

'When I was in that chair, I was void of emotion. It was as if I was watching myself and wasn't really there. Time went so fast and I don't recall a single thing I said or did. I played on instinct and had no intention of going to the end. All I knew is I wanted to keep back box 3 because that's the day my daughter Ria was born – and that's the one I opened second to last that contained the 1p! I thought about accepting the Banker's £25,000 offer, but I am impulsive… My sister came out from the audience and held on to me while Noel opened my box for me – and there was £50,000. I was numb, but I remember hugging my sister, before it all became a blur. It just didn't sink in.'

Starting box
No 11, containing
£50,000

Blues cruise 3

Red run 3

Banker offers
£4,000, £6,000,
£9,000, £13,000,
£5,000, £25,000

Swap or no swap?
No swap

Deal or No Deal?
No deal

Sajela takes home £50,000

NOEL'S VERDICT

'Sajela was a very pretty girl with laughing eyes that weakened The Banker's knees! What a great result.'

BACK TO REAL LIFE

What's the first thing you did when you got home?
'My dad picked me up at New Street station, brought me home and then I screamed and jumped up and down for joy. I was like a new person. It was such an emotional experience I felt as if I'd been on a pilgrimage of some kind.'

What did you do with the money?
'We're buying a three-bedroom house and I've invested it in the mortgage which will be paid off ten years earlier. That mortgage has felt like a weight on my shoulders, but now the pressure is off. Otherwise, I haven't spent a penny.'

Was the show life-changing?
'The mental experience changed my outlook on life and I've had so much luck since. I think the positivity of winning the money changes you. You're on a high all the time, and that's attracted more positive things into my life. For example, I've been promoted to manager.'

Any advice?
'Enjoy the experience. Don't go in with high expectations, then everything you get is a bonus.'

120

CONTESTANT

Name Matthew Scott
Broadcast 21st March 2006

THE GAME

Starting box No 5 containing £35,000
Banker offers £8,500, £16,000, £22,500, £20,000, £10,000, £22,450
Swap or no swap? No swap
Deal or No Deal? No deal

Matthew takes home £35,000

121

CONTESTANT

Name Marilyn Callum
Broadcast 22nd March 2006

THE GAME

Starting box No 7, containing £20,000
Banker offers £1,400, £6,500, £8,100, £9,500, £4,000, £5,500
Swap or no swap? No swap
Deal or No Deal? Deal!

Marilyn takes home £5,500

122

CONTESTANT

Name Dave Cheeseman
Broadcast 23rd March 2006

THE GAME

Starting box No 15, containing £50,000
Banker offers £5,000 £1,000, £8,400, £20,000
Swap or no swap? No swap
Deal or No Deal? Deal!

Dave takes home £20,000

123

CONTESTANT

Name Alison Toulouse-Lisle
Broadcast 24th March 2006

THE GAME

Starting box No 18, containing £10
Banker offers £1,200, £4,300, £3,800, £2,500, £5,100
Swap or no swap? No swap
Deal or No Deal? Deal!

Alison takes home £5,100

PERSONAL FILE

124

Name Nancy Englefield
Broadcast 25th March 2006
Occupation Retired primary school headteacher
Star sign Virgo
Eye colour Blue
Favourite number 8
Crisp flavour Ready salted
Favourite tipple Champagne

"I started watching one day by accident but became fascinated by this programme with Noel Edmonds and people with red boxes, and carried on watching until the end. I thought, 'I'd like to do that'. It's not one of those quizzes or game shows where you get asked stupid questions or are likely to show yourself up (even though most of my ex-pupils are fully grown up now, I don't want them seeing me making a fool of myself!)."

"On the day the call came to tell me that I'd been invited to take part, my daughter happened to be visiting me – all the way from Istanbul. It's fortunate she was there because the surprise of getting the call took me unawares and she had to grab a pen and paper to write their instructions down! She came back again for a long weekend when the programme was aired – particularly nice for us as it was Mothering Sunday."

THE GAME

"I had a figure that was the sum I needed for my purposes – around £20,000 to £30,000. I've just moved to a smaller home and wanted to add a conservatory for dining and entertaining, and rather than risk losing that amount, I knew I ought to take it. I'm not a greedy person, and it would have been a waste, I'd have probably given the excess away!"

Starting box No 21, containing £1
Blues cruise 4
Red run 3
Banker offers £2,000, £7,000, £4,700, £18,500
Swap or no swap? No swap
Deal or No Deal? Deal!

Nancy takes home £18,500

125

CONTESTANT

Name Nicholas Lee
Broadcast 27th March 2006

THE GAME

Starting box No 21, containing £50
Banker offers £6,700, £11,200, £3,600, £7,000, £4,900, £6,000
Swap or no swap? No swap
Deal or No Deal? Deal!

Nick takes home £6,000

126

CONTESTANT

Name Bob Thornthwaite
Broadcast 28th March 2006

THE GAME

Starting box No 22, containing £250,000
Banker offers £900, £350, £7,000, £18,500, £27,000
Swap or no swap? No swap
Deal or No Deal? Deal!

Bob takes home £27,000

127

CONTESTANT

Name Aaron Bell
Broadcast 29th March 2006

THE GAME

Starting box No 18, containing 50p
Banker offers £15,000, £30,000, £12,000, £25,000
Swap or no swap? No swap
Deal or No Deal? Deal!

Aaron takes home £25,000

DID YOU KNOW?

CAPRICORN is the highest-winning star sign

CONTESTANT

Name Lucy Harrington
Broadcast 30th March 2006

THE GAME

Starting box No 5, containing £5
Banker offers £50, £6,050, £1,800, £3,500, £7,500, £2,500
Swap or no swap? No swap
Deal or No Deal? No deal

Lucy takes home £5

128

CONTESTANT

Name Janet Rainbow King
Broadcast 31st March 2006

THE GAME

Starting box No 1, containing £1
Banker offers £6,100, £2,300, £7,000, £14,000, £400, £250
Swap or no swap? No swap
Deal or No Deal? No deal

Janet takes home £1

129

CONTESTANT

Name Steven Brown
Broadcast 1st April 2006

THE GAME

Starting box No 4, containing £750
Banker offers £800, £6,100, £13,005, £4,000, £1,305, £7,000
Swap or no swap? No swap
Deal or No Deal? Deal!

Steven takes home £7,000

130

131

CONTESTANT

Name James Hughes
Broadcast 3rd April 2006

THE GAME

Starting box No 10, containing 10p
Banker offers £5,500, £900,
£8,000. £9,900
Swap or no swap? No swap
Deal or No Deal? Deal!

James takes home £9,900

132

Grey-eyed Piscean **Kirsty Hardle**
reduced The Banker almost to tears
when she just about snatched the big
one. In the end, it escaped her grasp
but she still took home a meaty
£75,000. Read her story overleaf.

133

CONTESTANT

Name Johnnie Nickolls
Broadcast 5th April 2006

THE GAME

Starting box No 16, containing
£100,000
Banker offers £6,600, £2,800,
£8,300
Swap or no swap? No swap
Deal or No Deal? Deal!

Johnnie takes home £8,300

134

CONTESTANT

Name Sandra Tyler
Broadcast 6th April 2006

THE GAME

Starting box No 4, containing
£100,000
Banker offers £3,100, £8,900,
£14,200, £9,900, £12,900
Swap or no swap? No swap
Deal or No Deal? Deal!

Sandra takes home £12,900

135

CONTESTANT
Name Helen Evans
Broadcast 7th April 2006

THE GAME
Starting box No 8, containing £1,000
Banker offers £9,300, £6,100, £15,000, £22,000
Swap or no swap? No swap
Deal or No Deal? Deal!

Helen takes home £22,000

136

CONTESTANT
Name John Todd
Broadcast 8th April 2006

THE GAME
Starting box No 7, containing £20,000
Banker offers £4,001, £11,200, £19,500, £31,000, £39,000
Swap or no swap? No swap
Deal or No Deal? Deal!

John takes home £39,000

137

CONTESTANT
Name Pat Gregory
Broadcast 10th April 2006

THE GAME
Starting box No 8, containing £50
Banker offers £5,400, £14,000, £8,100 ,£5,500, £16,500
Swap or no swap? No swap
Deal or No Deal? Deal!

Pat takes home £16,500

29% of contestants went to university

THE WALK OF WEALTH

PERSONAL FILE

Name
Kirsty Hardle

Broadcast
4th April 2006

Occupation
Assistant psychologist

Star sign
Pisces

Eye colour
Grey

Favourite number
22

Crisp flavour
Thai sweet chilli

Favourite tipple
Tia Maria and coke

BEFORE THE SHOW

'I wanted to win about £15,000 - £10,000 to pay off debts and £5,000 for a boob job I'd been dreaming of since I was about 16. I'm very flat-chested and that had affected my confidence growing up. And I also wanted to have some fun and meet some interesting people.

'The timing was amazing for me. I was getting married to Daniel on the Saturday after the first week on the show. Everyone was fantastic: they did a collection and organised a mini hen night with lots of presents, and some of the guys even did a strip! After the wedding, everyone had a week off, then we came back and on the Wednesday the spotlight fell on me. I was feeling refreshed and raring to go...'

THE GAME

'It felt quite surreal, as if it wasn't me playing. I didn't have a game plan – I just wanted to play to the end and make the game as entertaining as possible. I had a good feeling about my box, but not necessarily that it contained the big one. The game went brilliantly, and the offers kept going up. The last two boxes were £250,000 and £75,000 – and The Banker offered me £125,000. I was having such a good time I didn't want it to end, so I turned it down. The adrenalin rush was amazing. Daniel was in the audience and The Banker spoke to him, saying there was only one person there luckier than me and that was him because he was married to me! Then he offered me a swap, but my lucky number was 22, my own box, so I refused. When the swap turned out to be the £250,000, I was gutted! Then you think, £75,000 is an believable sum, I'm so lucky.'

BANKER'S VERDICT

'The Hardle. She could have been the one. If she'd accepted the swap she would have taken me for... everything. I don't wish to discuss her a moment longer. Sometimes late at night, I see her face too. And her legs...'

Starting box
No 22, containing
£75,000

Blues cruise 7

Red run 4

Banker offers
£4,100, £11,000,
£17,000, £22,000,
£51,000,
£125,000

Swap or no swap?
Declined

Deal or No Deal?
No deal

Kirsty takes home £75,000

NOEL'S VERDICT

'Kirsty made it clear she only wanted £15,000 at the start of the show. However, her game had the most extraordinary turnaround and she held out for bigger and bigger offers, which was astonishing to witness! I am so glad that her approach paid off.'

BACK TO REAL LIFE

What's the first thing you did when you got home?
'Went shopping. Then called the hospital to get a consultation for my operation.'

What did you do with the money?
'Had the boob job – it's given me so much more confidence – helped my brother do his CBT bike test, and paid off our debts. What I value most is that if any of the family became ill, I have the money to help them.'

Was the show life-changing?
'Meeting the contestants restored my faith in human nature. I'd had a few bad experiences before: I was bullied at school, I'd recently been burgled and mugged. But the other players were so lovely and did so many kind things for me – organising my hen night and the whip round for my wedding – that it was one of the most momentous experiences of my life.'

Any advice?
'Make the most of it. It's a fantastic opportunity and if you can afford to be daring or risky, go for it.'

CONTESTANT

Name Peter Kaye

Broadcast 11th April 2006

THE GAME

Starting box No 8, containing £100

Banker offers £4,400, £8,800, £18,800, £20,000

Swap or no swap? No swap

Deal or No Deal? Deal!

Peter takes home £20,000

DID YOU KNOW?

Most contestants have 20:20 vision

CONTESTANT

Name Catherine Quinn

Broadcast 12th April 2006

THE GAME

Starting box No 1, containing £3,000

Banker offers £1,400, £4,700, £14,000, £7,470, £2,000, £8,000

Swap or no swap? No swap

Deal or No Deal? Deal!

Catherine takes home £8,000

CONTESTANT

Name Maxine Lewis

Broadcast 13th April 2006

THE GAME

Starting box No 5, containing £10,000

Banker offers £8,200, £2,200, £6,600, £6,100, £9,000, £2,900

Swap or no swap? No swap

Deal or No Deal? No deal

Maxine takes home £10,000

141

CONTESTANT
Name Fadil Osman
Broadcast 14th April 2006

THE GAME
Starting box No 6, containing 1p
Banker offers £1,700, £6,100, £6,100, £6,100, £3,050, £7,200
Swap or no swap? No swap
Deal or No Deal? No deal

Fadil takes home 1p

Fadil was the third contestant to gain entry to the exclusive 1p Club. He's left these shores to start a new life and unfortunately we have been unable to track him down. But we wish him the best of luck in all his future endeavours!

142

CONTESTANT
Name Gabrielle Hooker
Broadcast 15th April 2006

THE GAME
Starting box No 21, containing £50
Banker offers £1,500, £5,900, £700, £5,500, £6,500, £330
Swap or no swap? Swapped to Box 7, containing £1000
Deal or No Deal? No deal

Gabrielle takes home £2,000
(Banker doubled £1,000 as it was for charity)

CONTESTANT

Name Julia Morris
Broadcast 17th April 2006

THE GAME

Starting box No 20, containing £20,000

Banker offers £6,000, £7,800, £2,000, £5,800, £15,000, £17,500

Swap or no swap? Swapped to Box 10, containing £15,000

Deal or No Deal? No deal

Julia takes home £15,000

143

CONTESTANT

Name John Hogarth
Broadcast 18th April 2006

THE GAME

Starting box No 19, containing £75,000

Banker offers £2,800, £6,790, £4,900, £11,000, £18,000

Swap or no swap? No swap

Deal or No Deal? Deal!

John takes home £18,000

144

PERSONAL FILE

145

Name Linda Brown
Broadcast 19th April 2006
Occupation Volunteer bureau manager
Star sign Taurus
Eye colour Hazel
Favourite number 6 or 7
Favourite tipple Red wine

"I'd been on Ready, Steady, Cook, another Endemol show, and applied to audition for this one. I remember being taken straight to the studios from the train station to watch a show – the contestants came running in afterwards like wild people and I thought, "Arrgh, what have I let myself in for?" I did 23 shows before I went on, and it was so lovely building up friendships with everyone that I joked I'd become Noel's housekeeper and stay in that hotel for ever."

THE GAME

"I didn't have a game plan – it's sheer luck on the day – but you have to open five boxes to start with and I used my partner and daughters' birthdays. I felt like a duck on water – calm on the top but underneath paddling like mad. It was my 24th show, my birthday is on the 24th April, and I won £24,000, so maybe there is something in numbers."

"I didn't tell a soul the amount I won for six weeks until the show was aired. It drove them all mad but I wanted to watch their faces as they saw it unfolding on screen. The money was just a bonus - I spent it redoing my kitchen, gave my daughters a sum each, and we've booked a cruise to the Norwegian fjords next year."

Starting box No 20, containing £50,000
Blues cruise 5
Red run 3
Banker offers £321, £6,700, £9,000, £10,500, £24,000
Swap or no swap? No swap
Deal or No Deal? Deal!

Linda takes home £24,000

146

CONTESTANT

Name Gary Owen
Broadcast 20th April 2006

THE GAME

Starting box No 8, containing £5,000
Banker offers £7,000, £3,000, £10,000, £15,000, £29,999
Swap or no swap? No swap
Deal or No Deal? Deal!

Gary takes home **£29,999**

147

CONTESTANT

Name Michael Colclough
Broadcast 21st April 2006

THE GAME

Starting box No 21, containing £1,000
Banker offers £950, £600, £5,000, £10,000, £10,000
Swap or no swap? No swap
Deal or No Deal? Deal!

Michael takes home **£10,000**

PISCES is the second-highest winning star sign

148

CONTESTANT

Name James Thirkettle
Broadcast 22nd April 2006

THE GAME

Starting box No 9, containing £500
Banker offers £1,100, £8,000, £5,000, £3,000, £6,000, £2,000
Swap or no swap? No swap
Deal or No Deal? No deal

James takes home **£500**

149

CONTESTANT
Name Clare Barrett
Broadcast 24th April 2006

THE GAME
Starting box No 2, containing £250
Banker offers £9,000, £12,000, £17,000, £20,000, £8,000, £1,500
Swap or no swap? No swap
Deal or No Deal? Deal!

Clare takes home £1,500

150

Unlucky Dave Ellis joined the exclusive 1p Club on the 25th April 2006. Read his story overleaf.

151

CONTESTANT
Name Dorothy Hargreaves
Broadcast 7th February 2006

THE GAME
Starting box No 8, containing £1
Banker offers £6,700, £12,000, £3,300, £2,500, £3,100
Swap or no swap? No swap
Deal or No Deal? Deal!

Dorothy takes home £3,100

THE 1p CLUB

PERSONAL FILE

Name
Dave Ellis

Broadcast
25th April 2006

Occupation
Builder/plasterer

Star sign
Scorpio

Eye colour
Blue

Favourite number
8

Crisp flavour
Prawn cocktail

Favourite tipple
Best bitter

BANKER'S VERDICT

'Immovable. As if carved from very granite. Dave was a terrific gambler and could, in fact, have the makings of a Banker. Perhaps I'll grant him an audience…if he can scrape together the bus fare.'

BEFORE THE SHOW

'One of my daughters saw the show, and entered herself, my brother and me. Perhaps it's because I like cracking jokes and enjoy the limelight, but I was the only one who got through the audition. We'd agreed beforehand that we'd split any winnings three ways and I was going for £30,000 – £10,000 each. I wanted to help my daughter move out of a council flat and pay a bit towards her wedding and I wanted a good holiday too.

'The hotel was fabulous, better than the best holiday of my life! Every night the winners would put £300 each behind the bar and we'd drink until it was gone. I don't think I got to bed before 5.30am a single night. It took me a week afterwards to recover.'

THE GAME

'I lost a couple of big ones early and the game took away with me. I wanted £30,000 and so long as there was a bigger red than that on the board, I was going all the way. I'm a gambler and I bet on anything – dogs, horses, two flies going up a wall. To me this was like roulette, you're in and out of luck and no system in the world is going to help you. But being a gambler, I always expect to lose as well as win, so funnily enough when it started to go wrong I wasn't that disappointed.

'There comes a point when you want the penny, not a bigger sum – there's more fame to it. My brother Jez was in the audience and at the end we were on the floor laughing, relieved it was the penny and not the £5. At the hotel, people were more sorry for me than I was for myself, and lots of them were crying. It's a rollercoaster, up and down, and everyone wants you to win. I never cried but I was a bit disappointed. Still, I enjoyed every moment and if I had to do it all again, I'd play exactly the same way. I wouldn't change the experience for the world.'

Starting box
No 20, containing 1p

Blues cruise 3

Red run 4

Banker offers
£2,150, £5,150, £10,150, £1,150,
£1,000, £1.50

Swap or no swap?
No swap

Deal or No Deal?
No deal

Dave takes home 1p

NOEL'S VERDICT

'The Banker never offered anything much over £10,000 to Dave and so there were no real "tempters". These are the worst kind of games, but at least Dave can look back without regretting that he squandered a life-changing sum of money.'

BACK TO REAL LIFE

What was the first thing you did when you got home?
'I'd been away for a few weeks and there was a lot of work piled up. A firm I'd been working for had gone bankrupt and their cheque bounced, so I wasn't in a good financial way. But I soon got back on my feet.'

What did you do with the money?
'My daughter has blown up a picture of me shaking hands with Noel and framed it with the cheque. People have offered me thousands for that cheque, but I'm keeping it.'

Was the show life-changing?
'It was an eye-opener seeing the team on the show do jobs they really like. It made me think "Enough chasing money and work I don't enjoy." I packed in the building game and moved to a lovely spacious flat at the edge of a forest, overlooking a lake, doing maintenance for a conference centre. It's more relaxing, and now I'm doing something I enjoy.'

Any advice?
'Just get a figure in mind and don't think you're going to win the jackpot. Think of it as real money up there – there's a temptation to throw it all away.'

PERSONAL FILE

Name Richard Whitehurst
Broadcast 27th April 2006
Occupation Recruitment consultant
Star sign Aries
Eye colour Blue
Favourite number 14
Crisp flavour Cheese and onion
Favourite tipple Lager

"You go through the entire run of human emotions – it's a real rollercoaster...plus with the drinking and the partying into the evening, it was more exciting than any holiday I've ever been on. Life's not been the same since, not because of the prize money, but the experience of the show. In fact, I resigned from my job because life's too short to go back... I've got a couple of agents and found a bit of work as a TV extra and I'm looking into doing a few other things as well."

THE GAME

"I had no strategy. I saved two numbers to the end – my little girl and I have the same birthday date, the 14th, but other than that I picked the boxes of the newest contestants so they could get it out of the way. Funnily enough, I did have a figure in mind – £10,000 of obligations and £3,000 fun money to spend on holiday, so when £13,000 came up, I was not letting that go!"

Starting box No 2, containing £50
Blues cruise 4
Red run 3
Banker offers £1,313, £12,000, £3,100, £13,000
Swap or no swap? No swap
Deal or No Deal? Deal!

Richard takes home £13,000

Intrepid **Hilary Collins** refused all The Banker's offers and found that her box contained a fabulous £50,000. Read her story overleaf.

153

PERSONAL FILE

154

Name Massimo Dimambro
Broadcast 29th April 2005
Occupation City guardian
Star sign Sagittarius
Eye colour Blue
Favourite number 13
Crisp flavour Salt and vinegar
Favourite tipple Bacardi and coke

"On holiday in Italy I saw this game show called 'Affari Tuoi' – 'Your Business' – that everybody was watching. It looked fabulous fun, so I put my name down for it. Got home and switched on the TV to see a trailer for a new show, Deal or No Deal, that was starting in Britain. That's got to be an omen, I thought, so I applied. I didn't have any illusions about winning the big one, but I was in financial difficulties at the time so I was playing for a reason. Plus my dad wasn't well and I wanted to do something nice for him."

THE GAME

"It started superbly and I took out nearly all the blues. Everyone was incredibly excited – so excited that Tom's big belt buckle caught the edge of his box and sent it flying across the floor. I looked at Noel, he looked at me – nobody had a clue what to do. In the end, the game was stopped. In the rules, it says that if a game is interrupted it has to be started from scratch – but my board was phenomenal, so it was decided to continue after jiggling up the numbers in the remaining boxes. But now there was a voice in my head saying, this is jinxed! The Banker offered £16,000, I was tempted, asked the audience, who said No deal! I carried on, but the next boxes were the £250,000 and the £100,000. In the end I dealt for £7,400. It was heartbreaking – I felt as if my game had been snatched away. Now I'm going down in history as the 'first quarter-millionaire who never was'. Unless, of course, I get a recall..."

Starting box No 6, containing £15,000
Blues cruise 5
Red run 3
Banker offers £8,800, £16,000, £4,000, £7,400
Swap or no swap? No swap
Deal or No Deal? Deal!

Massimo takes home £7,400

THE WALK OF WEALTH

PERSONAL FILE

Name
Hilary Collins

Broadcast
28th April 2006

Occupation
Livery yard manager

Star sign
Pisces

Eye colour
Hazel

Favourite number
9

Pet owner
Yes

Crisp flavour
Chicken

Favourite tipple
Whisky

BANKER'S VERDICT

'Quite extraordinary. I became so concerned with identifying the contents of her little black bag, I failed to spot that she was one of the bravest players I have ever faced. Furthermore, she gave all her winnings to her daughters. Quite something.'

BEFORE THE SHOW

'To be honest, I'd never seen the show and even in the audition stage I didn't get the rules – but what I did understand was that there's £250,000 up for grabs and I wanted to be the first person to win the lot! Lifewise, I've had a few dismal years but in the last 12 months my fortunes turned and the show came towards the end, or the peak, rather, of my lucky year! I've always been around horses but for a long time I'd worked as a nurse with a small livery yard on the side. There were redundancies at work, and I took a settlement and opened my own stables. When I got the call, my aim was to win enough to set my daughters up on the property ladder.

'Meeting everyone was great – people were so supportive and they've all got a story to tell. It was like being on opposite shifts to my normal life – with the horses I'm early to bed and early to rise, this was adrenalin and late nights… I was exhausted to begin with! When you go up to the chair – and I'd had an inkling because I'd been there for a while – it's still one hell of a shock! Everything drops through the floor. It's no longer a show. As Noel says, this is your show now.'

THE GAME

'There's a little black book in which you write the life-changing things the money might bring for you. I didn't write anything but placed two keys – to represent houses for the girls – in it.

'I've been told I've got the biggest balls they've had on the show. I think everyone was quite amazed by my guts because I was this little country mouse who beat The Banker. I knew I had the £50,000 in my box. I had a vision and would have bet my house on it. When Noel gave me the offer of £21,000, I knew I had more than that in front of me. I wasn't intimidated by The Banker. In fact, I got a kick out of not letting him beat me into submission and accepting less. All the time there was a voice saying, "Don't worry, Hilary, You've got the 50 grand." And that turned out to be right.'

NOEL'S VERDICT

'What incredible self-belief Hilary had. She never wavered, always confident that she had a large sum of money. This is a dangerous tactic, but in Hilary's case it paid off handsomely!'

Starting box
No 18, containing
£50,000

Blues cruise 4

Red run 3

Banker offers
£10,000, £7,500,
£17,500, £9,000,
£21,000, £15,000

Swap or no swap?
No swap

Deal or No Deal?
No deal

Hilary takes home £50,000

BACK TO REAL LIFE

What's the first thing you did when you got home?
'I made sure my stables were still standing – I'd been away for two weeks! I then told the girls they could start looking at houses. Then we all got together and had some bubbly!'

What did you do with the money?
'As well as giving the girls their deposits, I threw a big barn dance for all my friends and we had a Deal or No Deal cake with a picture of Noel on it. I could also finally afford a horse of my very own which I've always wanted.'

Was the show life-changing?
'The money has improved the girls' lives, and given them an independence they wouldn't otherwise have. And I have Teddy, my horse – I decided not to call him Noel! It's a very special relationship with your own horse, and I'm very happy, and hope the dismal years are a thing of the past.'

Any advice?
'You're not gambling, you haven't put a stake down, you haven't "lost" anything, so don't worry and enjoy it. If I hadn't had my vision, I would easily have taken the £21,000 and been happy about it.'

155

CONTESTANT

Name Francesca Trezzi

Broadcast 1st May 2006

THE GAME

Starting box No 9, containing £50

Banker offers £9,500, £5,000, £17,000, £8,000, £20,000

Swap or no swap? No swap

Deal or No Deal? Deal!

Francesca takes home £20,000

156

Blue-eyed Piscean **Gary 'Gaz' Hall** played his game to a tee and took home the life-changing £100,000 that was in his box! Read his story overleaf.

157

CONTESTANT

Name Pat Miller

Broadcast 3rd May 2006

THE GAME

Starting box No 1, containing £1,000

Banker offers £9,500, £12,900, £17,500, £8,000, £500, £350

Swap or no swap? No swap

Deal or No Deal? No deal

Pat takes home £1,000

158

CONTESTANT

Name Patrick Roe

Broadcast 4th May 2006

THE GAME

Starting box No 4, containing £10,000

Banker offers £ 3,800, £10,000, £6,500, £800, £2,000, £3,000

Swap or no swap? No swap

Deal or No Deal? Deal!

Patrick takes home £3,000

DID YOU KNOW?

The lowest total payout in a single week was **£39,364.02**

159

CONTESTANT

Name Sandy Standen
Broadcast 5th May 2006

THE GAME

Starting box No 7, containing £20,000

Banker offers £4,300, £9,400, £3,500, £11,000

Swap or no swap? No swap

Deal or No Deal? Deal!

Sandy takes home £11,000

160

CONTESTANT

Name Morris Simpson
Broadcast 6th May 2006

THE GAME

Starting box No 16, containing £20,000

Banker offers £4,590, £9,000, £12,500, £10,000, £29,000, £101,000

Swap or no swap? Declined

Deal or No Deal? No deal

Morris takes home £20,000

161

CONTESTANT

Name Emma Dixon
Broadcast 8th May 2006

THE GAME

Starting box No 8, containing 10p

Banker offers £7,900, £10,000, £10,000, £14,000

Swap or no swap? No swap

Deal or No Deal? Deal!

Emma takes home £14,000

THE WALK OF WEALTH

PERSONAL FILE

Name
Gary 'Gaz' Hall

Broadcast
2nd May 2006

Occupation
Ice-cream parlour owner

Star sign
Pisces

Eye colour
Blue

Favourite number
13

Crisp flavour
Beef

Favourite tipple
Ice cream milkshake

BANKER'S VERDICT

I suppose I ought to have anticipated that the ice-cream man would leave covered in hundreds of thousands. As cool as one of his cornets. But far harder to lick. Or fit in the freezer. I'd happily give it a go though.

BEFORE THE SHOW

'I sell ice-creams on the Isle of Wight and in December it's really quiet. I was at home doing the ironing, thinking about taking a part-time job to help us out because my wife Debbie works incredibly hard in her barber's shop. The kids were watching television when Deal or No Deal came on and I thought it looked brilliant, a good chance to win some money, so I applied.

'Two days later I got a call from Michelle saying come to an audition in Brighton. I was really nervous – I'd never done anything like this before – but I wanted to have a go. The show was filmed on my 40th birthday and Mark the warm-up guy got everyone in the audience to sing happy birthday. It was fantastic and really lifted my spirits. I felt everyone was behind me.'

THE GAME

'I had box 13, which felt lucky, and my daughter's lucky number is 14, so I opened number 14 first – and it was the £250,000. Things didn't get better and the first offer from The Banker was £1,099 - £1,000 plus a 99 flake! Tell him I put hundreds and thousands on them as well, I said to Noel! I felt very nervous and despairing: at one stage, I wanted to stop the game and get off the show, and I'm so grateful Noel and the audience kept me going. As Noel said, risk nothing and you risk everything, so I decided to keep going as long as the £100,000 was on the board. Towards the end I was offered a swap. Tom said he thought his box contained the big one. And in my nervousness I said, 'Tom, I know you've got a big one, but mine's bigger than yours...' and the place erupted. When I opened my box and saw the £100,000, I just thought, is this for real? It sounds corny but you think it's a dream. I came out in shock.'

Starting box
No 13, containing
£100,000

Blues cruise 4

Red run 3

Banker offers
£1,099, £4,100,
£2,050, £3,000,
£8,200, £35,000

Swap or no swap?
Declined

Deal or No Deal?
No deal

Gary takes home
£100,000

NOEL'S VERDICT

'Gary seemed to grow in confidence and stature before our eyes. It really was a case of someone totally enjoying his moment in the crazy chair and I love the fact that his experience changed not only his personal life but also his commercial circumstances.'

BACK TO REAL LIFE

What's the first thing you did when you got home?
'Debbie and I had a secret giggle. I come from a modest background and £100,000 is a lot.'

What did you do with the money?
'I bought an old-fashioned ice-cream van. The idea is to grow the business by taking the ice-cream parlour on the road to all the outdoor events on the island. We were also building our own house with borrowed money, and it's helped towards that.'

Was the show life-changing?
'Now I get recognised wherever I go. Once, even in some grotty gents' urinals someone two feet away said, hey weren't you on Deal or No Deal? It was a bit embarrassing. People come up and ask to be photographed with me, or would I talk to their mum on their mobile. I find I can't be miserable any more: I've always been a happy person, but I've got happier and it's not the money, it's the experience. I'm very grateful.'

Any advice?
'Hold your nerve. It's annoying when people deal early – be courageous, follow your heart and go for it.'

Box 16 is the unluckiest box –
£250,000 has appeared in it
the least times

162

CONTESTANT

Name Theresa Borg
Broadcast 9th May 2006

THE GAME

Starting box No 1, containing
£15,000

Banker offers £6,100, £9,000,
£5,000, £20,000, £10,000, £3,800

Swap or no swap? No swap

Deal or No Deal? Deal!

Theresa takes home **£3,800**

163

CONTESTANT

Name Dave Wynn
Broadcast 10th May 2006

THE GAME

Starting box No 17, containing £100

Banker offers £800, £5,001,
£5,000, £10,000, £18,000

Swap or no swap? No swap

Deal or No Deal? Deal!

Dave takes home **£18,000**

164

CONTESTANT

Name Gary Marshall
Broadcast 11th May 2006

THE GAME

Starting box No 19 containing £3,000

Banker offers £7,000, £14,000,
£14,000, £21,000, £210, £1,400

Swap or no swap? Swapped to Box
16, containing £1

Deal or No Deal? No deal

Gary takes home **£1**

165

CONTESTANT

Name Susie Bowler
Broadcast 12th May 2006

THE GAME

Starting box No 20, containing 10p
Banker offers £5,000, £1,000, £10,000, £2,800, £6,125
Swap or no swap? No swap
Deal or No Deal? Deal!

Susie takes home £6,125

166

CONTESTANT

Name Maxine Biddiscombe
Broadcast 13th May 2006

THE GAME

Starting box No 18, containing £500
Banker offers £8,800, £2,200, £5,500, £3,300, £7,700
Swap or no swap? No swap
Deal or No Deal? Deal!

Maxine takes home £7,700

167

CONTESTANT

Name Simon Stanley
Broadcast 15th May 2006

THE GAME

Starting box No 15, containing £35,000
Banker offers £5,000, £7,700, £5,600, £4,500, £2,100, £13,000
Swap or no swap? No swap
Deal or No Deal? Deal!

Simon takes home £13,000

168

CONTESTANT

Name Armandtan Kent
Broadcast 16th May 2006

THE GAME

Starting box No 20, containing £5
Banker offers £7,400, £2,000, £4,700, £1,700, £1,020, £1.99
Swap or no swap? No swap
Deal or No Deal? No deal

Armandtan takes home £5

169

CONTESTANT
Name Sarah Monk
Broadcast 17th May 2006

THE GAME
Starting box No 12, containing £20,000

Banker offers £9,000, £4,000, £15,000, £50,000, £6,000

Swap or no swap? No swap

Deal or No Deal? Deal!

Sarah takes home £6,000

170

CONTESTANT
Name Tom Grimes
Broadcast 18th May 2006

THE GAME
Starting box No 14, containing £5

Banker offers £6,000, £18,000, £4,011, £11,000, £33,000

Swap or no swap? No swap

Deal or No Deal? Deal!

Tom takes home £33,000

DID YOU KNOW?

6% of contestants don't drink either tea or coffee

171

CONTESTANT
Name Raj Parmer
Broadcast 19th May 2006

THE GAME
Starting box No 8, containing £1

Banker offers £5,200. £10,400, £6,600, £320, £640, £64

Swap or no swap? No swap

Deal or No Deal? No deal

Raj takes home £1

172

CONTESTANT

Name Emma Bradley
Broadcast 20th May 2006

THE GAME

Starting box No 3, containing £5,000

Banker offers £2,000, £850,
£4,800, £1,800, £500, £2,000

Swap or no swap? No swap

Deal or No Deal? No deal

Emma takes home £5,000

173

CONTESTANT

Name Jason Von Wilgeroth
Broadcast 22nd May 2006

THE GAME

Starting box No 17, containing £750

Banker offers £1,400, £2,800,
£1,999, £5,000, £950, £300

Swap or no swap? No swap

Deal or No Deal? Deal!

Jason takes home £300

PERSONAL FILE

174

Name Michael 'Lofty' Lofthouse
Broadcast 23rd May 2006
Occupation Student/call centre worker
Star sign Libra
Eye colour Blue/green
Favourite number 4 and 18
Crisp flavour Prawn cocktail
Favourite tipple Jack Daniels

'I used to watch Deal or No Deal at university – all us students loved it. Then out of the blue one day, my girlfriend Katie announced she was pregnant. We were living with my mother, but thought it would be brilliant to win some money on DOND so we could put a deposit down on our own place. I thought £10,000 would be enough, I wasn't bothered about winning more – you go in with nothing so anything's a bonus.'

THE GAME

'My favourite number is 18, and my football shirt is a 4 in honour of Leeds United's Billy Bremner, so I planned to keep those two numbers until last. Just before the show my friend Simon gave me a baby's top with 'My Daddy beat the Banker' printed on it. Being in that chair was nervewracking but I felt ecstatic. I've got a strong Leeds accent and Noel kept counting how many times I shouted 'Come on' every time a box was opened. It was a brilliant game and I took away lots of small numbers at the beginning. Then I got offered £18,000 by The Banker and thought I just can't afford to lose this – so I dealt! Now Olivia May is four months old and we're just about to get our first mortgage. It couldn't have worked out better...'

Starting box No 12, containing 50p
Blues cruise 3
Red run 6
Banker offers £9,400, £6,000, £18,000
Swap or no swap? No swap
Deal or No Deal? Deal!

Michael takes home £18,000

175

CONTESTANT

Name Patricia Kirkup-Sykes
Broadcast 24th May 2006

THE GAME

Starting box No 2, containing £250,000

Banker offers £6,300, £9,000, £14,500, £8,500, £32,000

Swap or no swap? No swap

Deal or No Deal? Deal!

Patricia takes home £32,000

176

CONTESTANT

Name Richard Pow
Broadcast 25th May 2006

THE GAME

Starting box No 21, containing £100

Banker offers £3,900, £10,000, £5,146, £8,500, £20,000

Swap or no swap? No swap

Deal or No Deal? Deal!

Richard takes home £20,000

177

CONTESTANT

Name June Furbey
Broadcast 26th May 2006

THE GAME

Starting box No 7, containing 50p

Banker offers £3,700, £9,000, £14,000, £23,000

Swap or no swap? No swap

Deal or No Deal? Deal!

June takes home £23,000

SCORPIO is the fifth-highest winning star sign

178

CONTESTANT

Name Mark Fong
Broadcast 27th May 2006

THE GAME

Starting box No 20, containing £5,000

Banker offers £10,000, £20,000, £8,000, £6,000, £9,000, £5,000

Swap or no swap? No swap

Deal or No Deal? No deal

Mark takes home £5,000

179

CONTESTANT

Name Simone Lazarus
Broadcast 29th May 2006

THE GAME

Starting box No 19, containing £1

Banker offers £5,500. £15,000, £10,000, £18,000, £25,500, £15,500, £75,000

Swap or no swap? No swap

Deal or No Deal? No deal

Simone takes home £1

180

CONTESTANT

Name Colin Beckwith
Broadcast 30th May 2006

THE GAME

Starting box No 15, containing £250

Banker offers £2,200, £4,400, £5,800, £3,300, £10,000

Swap or no swap? No swap

Deal or No Deal? Deal!

Colin takes home £10,000

CONTESTANT

Name Fran Taylor

Broadcast 31st May 2006

THE GAME

Starting box Box 22, containing £75,000

Banker offers £7,900, £3,100, £10,000, £5,000, £28,000

Swap or no swap? No swap

Deal or No Deal? Deal!

181

Fran takes home £28,000

CONTESTANT

Name John 'Buzz' Busby

Broadcast 1st June 2006

THE GAME

Starting box No 21, containing £100

Banker offers £514, £1,915, £4,000, £8,200, £9,800

Swap or no swap? No swap

Deal or No Deal? Deal!

182

John takes home £9,800

CONTESTANT

Name Cynthia 'Stevie' Saggers

Broadcast 2nd June 2006

THE GAME

Starting box No 12, containing £3,000

Banker offers £7,007, £5,000, £14,000, £21,056, £11,000, £1,300

Swap or no swap? No swap

Deal or No Deal? Deal!

183

Cynthia takes home £1,300

CONTESTANT
Name Suresh Rowe 'Jainie'
Broadcast 3rd June 2006

THE GAME
Starting box No 18, containing £100
Banker offers £9,100, £9,100, £20,000, £31,000
Swap or no swap? No swap
Deal or No Deal? Deal!

Suresh takes home £31,000

CONTESTANT
Name James Brady
Broadcast 5th June 2006

THE GAME
Starting box No 19, containing £750
Banker offers £1,220, £8,000, £14,700
Swap or no swap? No swap
Deal or No Deal? Deal!

James takes home £14,700

Average winnings for those contestants who are bald: £28,700

PERSONAL FILE

186

Name Suzanne Akers
Broadcast 6th June 2006
Occupation Self-employed swimming teacher
Star sign Leo
Eye colour Blue
Favourite number 3
Crisp flavour Cheese and onion
Favourite tipple Coke or bitter lemon

"I'm not great at general knowledge, so I loved the idea of a non-quiz game show where you get together with a big group of people for a couple of weeks. It was a life-changing experience being in that hotel: I had the best time ever there, doing the hokey cokey every evening, and I made two great new friends, Drew and Jainie – now we speak every week."

THE GAME

"Nothing prepares you for that spotlight hitting you and Noel saying it's your turn – your legs go to jelly! Any game plan went out of my head instantly, but my lucky number is 3 and I knew I wanted Box 3. On my first round The Banker offered me a swap – the only time he'd ever done that – and I got my magic box. I was so happy and it gave me the confidence to take on The Banker and do him over 100 per cent! In the end he offered me £47,000 and I took it. I'm using the money to take the family out to the Canary Islands in December, and to buy a holiday home there."

Starting box No 19, containing £500
Blues cruise 3
Red run 5
Banker offers £7,000, £26,000, £47,000
Swap or no swap? Swapped to Box 3
Deal or No Deal? Deal!

Suzanne takes home £47,000

187

CONTESTANT

Name Drew McCririck
Broadcast 7th June 2006

THE GAME

Starting box No 20, containing £20,000

Banker offers £4,800, £12,000, £15,001, £25,000, £17,500

Swap or no swap? No swap

Deal or No Deal? Deal!

Drew takes home £17,500

LEO is the third-highest winning star sign

188

CONTESTANT

Name Becca Hossany
Broadcast 8th June 2006

THE GAME

Starting box No 13, containing £1,000

Banker offers £1,200, £9,200, £14,500, £20,000, £7,000, £250

Swap or no swap? No swap

Deal or No Deal? No deal

Becca takes home £1,000

189

CONTESTANT

Name Peter Temitope
Broadcast 9th June 2006

THE GAME

Starting box No 13, containing £1

Banker offers £1,900, £5,800, £2,200, £10,000, £25,000

Swap or no swap? No swap

Deal or No Deal? Deal!

Peter takes home £25,000

190

CONTESTANT

Name Joan Forrest

Broadcast 10th June 2006

THE GAME

Starting box No 6, containing 10p

Banker offers £8,000, £13,013, £20,000, £5,000, £2,999, £3,000

Swap or no swap? No swap

Deal or No Deal? No deal

Joan takes home 10p

191

CONTESTANT

Name Richard Hyams

Broadcast 11th June 2006

THE GAME

Starting box No 20, containing £75,000

Banker offers £100, £18,000, £4,000, £1,100, £6,100

Swap or no swap? No swap

Deal or No Deal? Deal!

Richard takes home £6,100

192

CONTESTANT

Name Louise Brand-Parkinson

Broadcast 12th June 2006

THE GAME

Starting box No 6, containing £15,000

Banker offers £850, £8,500, £19,000, £30,000

Swap or no swap? No swap

Deal or No Deal? Deal!

Louise takes home £30,000

193

CONTESTANT

Name Carlton Rhodes
Broadcast 12th June 2006

THE GAME

Starting box No 4, containing £10

Banker offers £7,000, £12,500,
£15,000, £4,000, £1,100, £200

Swap or no swap? No swap

Deal or No Deal? No deal

Carlton takes home £10

194

CONTESTANT

Name Darren Woolley
Broadcast 13th June 2006

THE GAME

Starting box No 22, containing £200

Banker offers £11,000, £7,500,
£13,500, £19,900

Swap or no swap? No swap

Deal or No Deal? Deal!

Darren takes home £19,900

AQUARIUS is the fourth-
lowest winning star sign

195

CONTESTANT

Name Joanne Curtis
Broadcast 13th June 2006

THE GAME

Starting box No 2, containing
£35,000

Banker offers £810, £7,500,
£12,500, £18,000, £31,000

Swap or no swap? No swap

Deal or No Deal? Deal!

Joanne takes home £31,000

196

CONTESTANT

Name Vanessa Gillen
Broadcast 14th June 2006

THE GAME

Starting box No 20, containing £10
Banker offers £5,013, £1,300, £1,300, £9,000, £13,000, £4,000
Swap or no swap? No swap
Deal or No Deal? No deal

Vanessa takes home £10

DID YOU KNOW?

Most contestants have brown hair

197

CONTESTANT

Name Scott Gardner
Broadcast 14th June 2006

THE GAME

Starting box No 20, containing £5
Banker offers £7,000, £17,000, £9,000, £3,100, £5,010, £7.10
Swap or no swap? No swap
Deal or No Deal? No deal

Scott takes home £5

198

CONTESTANT

Name Trevor Glenn
Broadcast 15th June 2006

THE GAME

Starting box No 19, containing £20,000
Banker offers £5,010, £10,005, £35,000, £25,000
Swap or no swap? No swap
Deal or No Deal? Deal!

John takes home £25,000

199

CONTESTANT

Name Teresa Hodges
Broadcast 15th June 2006

THE GAME

Starting box No 1, containing £10
Banker offers £8,000, £4,100, £8,000, £4,100, £2,500, £300
Swap or no swap? No swap
Deal or No Deal? No deal

Teresa takes home £10

200

CONTESTANT

Name Ron McBay
Broadcast 16th June 2006

THE GAME

Starting box No 8, containing £20,000
Banker offers £9,200, £1,200, £6,200, £13,200, £13,201, £5,200
Swap or no swap? No swap
Deal or No Deal? No deal

Ron takes home £20,000

201

CONTESTANT

Name Chrissie Brinton
Broadcast 16th June 2006

THE GAME

Starting box No 22, containing 50p
Banker offers £1,950, £10,000, £5,000, £5,700, £8,853
Swap or no swap? No swap
Deal or No Deal? Deal!

Chrissie takes home £8,853

202

CONTESTANT

Name Debbie Woodcock
Broadcast 17th June 2006

THE GAME

Starting box No 22, containing £250,000

Banker offers £9,000, £3,100, £12,000, £7,500, £15,000

Swap or no swap? No swap

Deal or No Deal? Deal!

Debbie takes home £15,000

CANCER is the second-lowest winning star sign

203

CONTESTANT

Name Lee Bentley
Broadcast 17th June 2006

THE GAME

Starting box No 21, containing £15,000

Banker offers £11,000, £16,500, £10,000, £10,001

Swap or no swap? No swap

Deal or No Deal? Deal!

Lee takes home £10,001

204

CONTESTANT

Name Frank Markin
Broadcast 18th June 2006

THE GAME

Starting box No 10, containing £35,000

Banker offers £50,000, £5,000, £2,500, £9,500, £20,000

Swap or no swap? No swap

Deal or No Deal? Deal!

Frank takes home £20,000

205

CONTESTANT

Name Eileen Bowater

Broadcast 19th June 2006

THE GAME

Starting box No 7, containing 50p

Banker offers £5,250, £1,250, £12,500, £16,500, £16,500

Swap or no swap? No swap

Deal or No Deal? Deal!

Eileen takes home £16,500

206

CONTESTANT

Name Yvonne Fitzpatrick

Broadcast 20th June 2006

THE GAME

Starting box No 16, containing £10,000

Banker offers £1,800, £7,000, £6,500, £1,500, £4,000,

Swap or no swap? No swap

Deal or No Deal? Deal!

Yvonne takes home £4,000

207

CONTESTANT

Name Wayne Lakin

Broadcast 21st June 2006

THE GAME

Starting box No 4, containing £250

Banker offers £999, £19,999, £9,999, £1,999, £999

Swap or no swap? No swap

Deal or No Deal? Deal!

Wayne takes home £999

DID YOU KNOW?

28% of contestants prefer coffee

208

CONTESTANT

Name Shirley Barry
Broadcast 22nd June 2006

THE GAME

Starting box No 16, containing £50,000
Banker offers £8,300, £16,000, £17,500, £21,000, £55,000, £20,000
Swap or no swap? No swap
Deal or No Deal? Deal!

Shirley takes home £20,000

209

CONTESTANT

Name Bianca Marshall
Broadcast 23rd June 2006

THE GAME

Starting box No 22, containing £50,000
Banker offers £5,000, £10,000, £3,800, £600, £2,000
Swap or no swap? No swap
Deal or No Deal? Deal!

Bianca takes home £2,000

210

CONTESTANT

Name Penelope Boston
Broadcast 24th June 2006

THE GAME

Starting box No 14, containing £10,000
Banker offers £1,313, £7,013, £11,012, £17,500, £25,000, £30,000
Swap or no swap? No swap
Deal or No Deal? Deal!

Penelope takes home £30,000

12

GEMINI is the lowest-winning star sign

211

CONTESTANT
Name Ryan Kerr
Broadcast 26th June 2006

THE GAME
Starting box No 15, containing £500
Banker offers £12,000, £4,000, £5,500, £15,500
Swap or no swap? No swap
Deal or No Deal? Deal!

Ryan takes home **£15,500**

212

CONTESTANT
Name Melanie Lucy
Broadcast 27th June 2006

THE GAME
Starting box No 22, containing £100
Banker offers £9,100, £15,500, £30,000
Swap or no swap? No swap
Deal or No Deal? Deal!

Melanie takes home **£30,000**

213

CONTESTANT
Name Ashok Kumar
Broadcast 28th June 2006

THE GAME
Starting box No 8, containing £250
Banker offers £7,000, £21,000, £12,000, £15,000, £2,500, £125
Swap or no swap? No swap
Deal or No Deal? No deal

Ashok takes home **£250**

214

CONTESTANT

Name Amy Phillips
Broadcast 29th June 2006

THE GAME

Starting box No 5, containing £5,000
Banker offers £6,600, £16,600, £20,000, £5,000, £9,950
Swap or no swap? No swap
Deal or No Deal? Deal!

Amy takes home £9,950

215

CONTESTANT

Name Mark Wilkes
Broadcast 30th June 2006

THE GAME

Starting box No 8, containing £10
Banker offers £2,400, £9,600, £17,000, £17,000, £10,000, £30,000
Swap or no swap? No swap
Deal or No Deal? Deal!

Mark takes home £30,000

216

CONTESTANT

Name Janelle Campbell
Broadcast 1st July 2006

THE GAME

Starting box No 15, containing 50p
Banker offers £5,000, £2,500, £12,000, £8,500, £3,000, £1,300
Swap or no swap? Swapped to Box 7, containing £5,000
Deal or No Deal? No deal

Janelle takes home £5,000

217

CONTESTANT

Name Paul Bridgewood
Broadcast 3rd July 2006

THE GAME

Starting box No 6, containing £1
Banker offers £13,000, £19,500, £9,500, £7,500, £17,000, £32,000
Swap or no swap? No swap
Deal or No Deal? Deal!

Paul takes home £32,000

218

CONTESTANT

Name Alan Jaye

Broadcast 4th July 2006

THE GAME

Starting box No 15, containing £1,000

Banker offers £6,000, £7,800, £6,000, £7,800, £2,400

Swap or no swap? No swap

Deal or No Deal? Deal!

Alan takes home £2,400

219

CONTESTANT

Name Linda Edwards

Broadcast 5th July 2006

THE GAME

Starting box No 11, containing £20,000

Banker offers £14,000, £11,000, £16,000, £20,000

Swap or no swap? No swap

Deal or No Deal? Deal!

Linda takes home £20,000

220

CONTESTANT

Name Victor Hammond

Broadcast 6th July 2006

THE GAME

Starting box No 6, containing £10

Banker offers £1,234, £9,000, £9,000, £9,000, £4,321, £19,000

Swap or no swap? No swap

Deal or No Deal? Deal!

Vic takes home £19,000

221

CONTESTANT

Name Roy Ribbans

Broadcast 7th July 2006

THE GAME

Starting box No 3, containing £15

Banker offers £7,500, £12,500, £3,500, £7,500, £27,500

Swap or no swap? No swap

Deal or No Deal? Deal!

Roy takes home £27,500

222

CONTESTANT

Name Nick Martin

Broadcast 8th July 2006

THE GAME

Starting box No 16, containing £250

Banker offers £7,700, £15,000, £10,000, £6,123, £5,001, £8,500

Swap or no swap? No swap

Deal or No Deal? Deal!

Nick takes home £8,500

46% of contestants prefer tea

223

CONTESTANT

Name Pierre Pozzuto

Broadcast 10th July 2006

THE GAME

Starting box No 18, containing £10

Banker offers £10,000, £18,000, £24,000, £7,000

Swap or no swap? No swap

Deal or No Deal? Deal!

Pierre takes home £7,000

224

CONTESTANT

Name Monica Waterman

Broadcast 11th July 2006

THE GAME

Starting box No 12, £15,000

Banker offers £8,012, £19,012, £20,012, £12,000

Swap or no swap? No swap

Deal or No Deal? Deal!

Monica takes home £12,000

PERSONAL FILE

225

Name Sue Hopper
Broadcast 12th July 2006
Occupation Housewife
Star sign Aries
Eye colour Blue
Favourite number 18
Pet owner Yes
Crisp flavour Plain
Favourite tipple Gin and Tonic

"I had a wonderful time and still watch. I've been into it from the beginning. My kids have had burnt tea or no tea for the past year because I was stuck in front of DOND. The three weeks – being with the other Names, and the crew, as well as doing the shows – goes down as truly one of the best experiences I've had in life, up there with being in the army, travelling the world, having kids even, honest!"

THE GAME

"On my turn, a little beetle landed on the podium…Noel christened him "Neil" and this gave rise to "Neil or no Neil?". I was offered £18,401 (the £1 was for the bug) and when I looked down, Neil was on his back with his legs in the air. "He's dead!" I said, and the camera panned in to show him. I thought "This is an omen, if Neil's dead, I should Deal!" And bugger me if he didn't then just wiggle his legs! I took that as a sign that Neil wanted me to carry on."

"When I took the offer of £8,401, I dithered for a long time, but Neil came over and crawled on a photo of my family and I thought "Just take it!" Mind you, if I'd have known he was going to cost me £10 grand, I would have stamped on him!"

Starting box No 16, containing £50,000
Blues cruise 2
Red run 3
Banker offers £6,400, £9,400, £12,400, £18,401, £8,401
Swap or no swap? No swap
Deal or No Deal? Deal!

Sue takes home £8,401

226

CONTESTANT

Name Lynda Birch

Broadcast 13th July 2006

THE GAME

Starting box No 19, containing £50

Banker offers £7,100, £4,000, £20,000

Swap or no swap? No swap

Deal or No Deal? Deal!

Lynda takes home £20,000

227

Unlucky atlantic-rower **Sally Kettle** refused all offers and became the first woman to enter the 1p Club. Read her story overleaf.

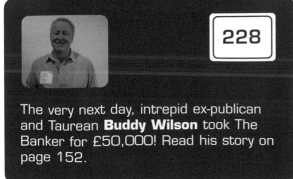

228

The very next day, intrepid ex-publican and Taurean **Buddy Wilson** took The Banker for £50,000! Read his story on page 152.

THE 1p CLUB

PERSONAL FILE

Name
Sally Kettle

Broadcast
14th July 2006

Occupation
Motivational speaker and ocean rower

Star sign
Pisces

Eye colour
Brown

Favourite number
8

Crisp flavour
Salt and vinegar

Favourite tipple
Whisky

BEFORE THE SHOW

'Before I went on, I'd rowed across the Atlantic, so there's not much fazes me! For me, though, it's all about the journey, the getting there, rather than the winning that's the important thing. It was much the same with Deal or No Deal. The experience was always going to be more interesting than the result. I didn't go to win huge amounts but, yes, I did have a figure in mind. £30,000 would be a life-changing amount in that it would pay off some debt and free me up to work on a book about ocean rowing.

'I don't think I'm a lucky person. But then I'm not unlucky either. Some things just happen…it's mostly down to fate and chance.'

THE GAME

'I based my decisions on a Transatlantic boat race I was in. There were boats numbered 1 to 22 in the competition so I eliminated the boxes in the same order the boats came in. I was completely calm and as I didn't get offered anything near my ideal sum, I held out. After the £18,800 offer, which I turned down, I thought, "It's going to go sky high… or plummet." If The Banker had gone up to say £25,000, I probably wouldn't have gambled it away but I thought, "I came to play the game, bring it on!" Past the £18,800 mark when the offers deteriorated, I did start to break down. I appreciate that Noel and The Banker didn't take the mick. The Banker spoke to me, actually, he said, "People like you don't need luck in life, you create your own. It's been a pleasure." And Noel was a total honey. That really meant a lot.'

BANKER'S VERDICT

'The lovely Sally Kettle. Or Copper Kettle as she is now known since her famous win. The first female member of the 1p Club and living proof that it takes the same amount of courage to win a penny as it will the quarter of a million. She's still row-rowing her boat gently down the stream, I believe; just not very merrily.'

Starting box
No 3, containing 1p

Blue cruise 4

Red run 3

Banker offers
£8,800, £18,800, £18,800, £1,829,
£1,111, 21p

Swap or no swap?
No swap

Deal or No Deal?
No deal

NOEL'S VERDICT

'Sally was a pleasure to have on the show, but unfortunately her tactics of choosing the boxes based on losing boats during a sailing trip didn't pay off!'

Sally takes home 1p

BACK TO REAL LIFE

What's the first thing you did when you got home?
'I burst into tears! Actually I cried like a kid for a couple of days. I'm over it now, but it was intense at the time – you can't walk away from a show like that and not be affected.'

What did you do with the money?
'The 1p cheque is sitting on my bedroom radiator. I still don't know what to do with it.'

Was the show life-changing?
'I'm a public speaker and do talks and motivation, team-building and so on. And I've got a great story now. I tell people that I've been on Deal or No Deal and ask them to guess how much I won - they never guess it's a penny and it makes people warm to you more than say several grand. I'm the first woman in the 1p Club, and I'm proud of it. I've taken the experience and turned it into something I wanted it to be.'

Any advice?
'It's difficult to say because I was upset at the time and thought I'd never go down that road again – but that's a lie, I would do it again tomorrow. You have to go for it. Seize the day!'

THE WALK OF WEALTH

PERSONAL FILE

Name
Buddy Wilson

Broadcast
15th July 2006

Occupation
Retired publican

Star sign
Taurus

Eye colour
Green

Favourite number
13

Crisp flavour
Peppercorn

Favourite tipple
Vodka

BANKER'S VERDICT

'Another spectacularly single-minded player, whom I was simply powerless to stop. This Buddy certainly can spare a dime now. Curse him.'

BEFORE THE SHOW

'I wanted 15 minutes of fame, I'd never had it and I thought, I'm 60 and I want to see myself on television. Not in a vain way, though sadly I looked a bit older than I thought I did, but for the experience. Being in the hotel was brilliant, I enjoyed the comradeship, and there was a party every night. At 10.30pm, 40 of us would do the hokey cokey in the high street, buses would stop, policemen were laughing and everyone would join in. I did 22 shows and standing with the boxes I was nervous every day. But when it was my turn to take centre stage, I felt like a showman. I could have conquered the world.'

THE GAME

'The night before I'd had a dream that 50 people had knocked on my door looking for The Banker, they'd searched my house but couldn't find him. The number 50 stuck in my head, and I wrote in Noel's book that I wanted to take away £50,000. But when I was playing I didn't think much about the money. In that spotlight you seem to float a little, and two hours passed in 10 minutes.

'I told Noel I wanted to savour every moment, and I did. I lost the £250,000 on my first box, number 2, and everyone was amazed when I turned down the £27,500 deal. At the end there were only two boxes left. The Banker offered me £50,000 and I took it. Now I get a cold sweat thinking, "One more box, and you'd have lost the lot," but at the time I felt like a million dollars. I enjoyed every second of the game.'

Starting box
No 19, containing
£3,000

Blues cruise 3

Red run 3

Banker offers
£1,300, £13,000,
£16,000, £13,000,
£27,500, £50,000

Swap or no swap?
No swap

Deal or No Deal?
Deal!

Buddy takes home
£50,000

NOEL'S VERDICT

'I really warmed to Buddy; no wonder he was a successful publican! He had a charm about him and we all really wanted him to win big money. The £50,000 he got was a brilliant result, especially considering the game started so badly.'

BACK TO REAL LIFE

What's the first thing you did when you got home?
'Pinched myself.'

What did you do with the money?
'I bought myself a big new plasma telly, some premium bonds, and am going on a cruise to Portugal and Gibraltar with my girlfriend. And I treated my three children. I didn't give them a cheque, but changed the money into notes, then went and threw it in the air for each of them. I'd always wanted to do that!'

Was the show life-changing?
'It's strange, but I feel much more confident. Being a publican you have to face up to situations so I've always been fairly confident. But standing up and speaking in front of millions on a television show made me feel so good. Though the withdrawal symptoms are dreadful…'

Any advice?
'Be careful – the game can run away from you so easily. Within three boxes it's gone. So go in with a figure in your mind that'll make a real change in your life. Then take it when it's offered.'

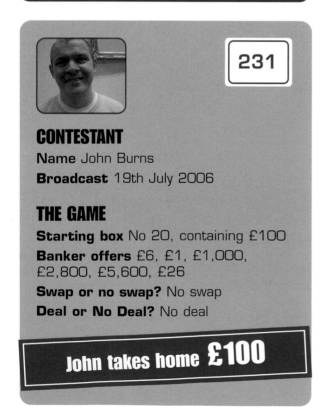

Connell Gibson's luck was against him when he swapped his box containing £10,000 for the one containing 1p! Read his story overleaf.

229

230

CONTESTANT
Name Debbie Crook
Broadcast 18th July 2006

THE GAME
Starting box No 8, containing £250
Banker offers £5,900, £3,142, £10,000.01, £5,000, £999, £99
Swap or no swap? No swap
Deal or No Deal? No deal

Debbie takes home £250

231

CONTESTANT
Name John Burns
Broadcast 19th July 2006

THE GAME
Starting box No 20, containing £100
Banker offers £6, £1, £1,000, £2,800, £5,600, £26
Swap or no swap? No swap
Deal or No Deal? No deal

John takes home £100

DID YOU KNOW?

LIBRA is the third-lowest winning star sign

232

CONTESTANT

Name Christine Bailey
Broadcast 20th July 2006

THE GAME

Starting box No 8, containing £50
Banker offers £2,700, £12,000, £18,000, £25,000
Swap or no swap? No swap
Deal or No Deal? Deal!

Christine takes home £25,000

233

CONTESTANT

Name Naqiyah Sadicot
Broadcast 21st July 2006

THE GAME

Starting box No 20, containing £20,000
Banker offers £7,777, £14,014, £4,949, £14,014
Swap or no swap? No swap
Deal or No Deal? Deal!

Naqiyah takes home £14,014

234

CONTESTANT

Name Giorgio Felicini
Broadcast 22nd July 2006

THE GAME

Starting box No 6, containing 1p
Banker offers £6,800, £3,400, £1,700, £425, £2,500, £25
Swap or no swap? No swap
Deal or No Deal? No deal

Giorgio takes home 1p

Giorgio Felicini made history – as the last player of the series and again when he became the 7th member of The 1p Club! Unfortunately, we have been unable to track him down, but wish him the best in his future endeavours.

THE 1p CLUB

PERSONAL FILE

Name
Connell Gibson

Broadcast
17th July 2006

Occupation
Warehouse delivery driver

Star sign
Gemini

Eye colour
Blue

Favourite number
7 or 9

Crisp flavour
Salt and vinegar

Favourite tipple
Lager

BANKER'S VERDICT

'Connell played the game wearing a shirt with the word "Courage" on the back. His performance proved the word might well have been written right through him like a stick of rock. Or maybe a penny chew.'

BEFORE THE SHOW

'If I got one of the big reds, I could pay off my mortgage, take care of my family (I'm a father of four) take us all on a big holiday... But more than anything I wanted the experience: it looked like a laugh and I was up for it! I reckon that I'm a lucky sort of person – I've got four lovely daughters and a beautiful wife, so yes, I am a lucky man.

'Deal or No Deal is its own world – you don't really know the feeling unless you've done it, you've been on the inside.. I was up until the early hours partying and bonding every night. I had the role of "Daddy", looking after the new contestants and making sure they were comfortable and okay – and I loved it, more than my game! I'm outgoing, I like a laugh, it suited me down to the ground.'

THE GAME

'My numbers were completely random, and on reflection maybe I should have had more of a game plan. The Banker's offers just didn't seem enough and then when I got the chance to swap I went for it. It was the only time you could say I'd gone with an intuition. I swapped my box for one that had my "lucky number" on it – clearly not that lucky – and swapped £10,000 for 1p!

'I wasn't the only one. When I was there Sally and later Giorgio got 1p boxes and, of course, you think, "Why them? They're so nice!" But when it happens to you, you have to think it comes down to chance. It's one of those things.'

Starting box
No 22, containing £10,000

Blues cruise 4

Red run 4

Banker offers
£6,600, £13,200, £18,004.50,
£9,000, £900, £2,000

Swap or no swap?
Swapped to box 7, containing 1p

Deal or No Deal?
No deal

Connell takes home 1p

NOEL'S VERDICT
'The swap is The Banker's most dangerous trap and unfortunately Connell fell into it.'

BACK TO REAL LIFE

What's the first thing you did when you got home?
'I went back to work! Fortunately, I couldn't tell anyone what I'd won and had to keep it a secret. I was pretty bloody glad of that! Straight after the show though, I was still "Daddy" so I had to do speeches, introductions and that was good because it took my mind off it. I also couldn't possibly have drunk more – I definitely drowned my sorrows!'

What did you do with the money?
'No I haven't spent it because I haven't seen anything I want yet! Seriously though, the wife's lost the cheque tidying up – bet she wouldn't have done that if it was for £1,000!'

Was the show life-changing?
'I've got a small bit of fame out of it. I still get recognised... I've just joined my local football team and the crowd chucked loads of 1ps at me during my first match! But I tell you what, I picked each and every one of them up and there was £2.50. I ordered a pint saying, "You'll have to count them!"'

Any advice?
'Do it! Grasp every minute because it just flies by. But if you've got a figure in mind and you get anywhere near it, take it because it might not come around again.'

THE DEAL OR NO DEAL DICTIONARY

1p Club, The This select group of seven (from the first series) are led by Nick Bain, who became the founding member when he left the show with the lowest number on the board – 1p. In the way of such things, admittance to this choice band of contestants has become rather sought after by certain players. There are those who would rather have the cachet and infamy of winning 1p, than a middling amount of money, such as £100.

22, The This is the exact number of boxes that line up in every Deal or No Deal, and so represents the number of contestants who play in each game. Each box has a different sum of money, just as each contestant has a different method of doing the hokey cokey.

Banker, The The omnipotent, enigmatic figure without whom, he would have you believe, there is no Deal or No Deal. And he's probably right. See Chapter 3, an Interview with The Banker.

Big One, The; AKA Big Boy, The The largest amount of money that any player can win, if they play their boxes and The Banker right: £250,000. In used fivers (actually, it's a cheque). Strangely, the Big One is not necessarily the reason that everyone plays the game. Many contestants set their sights much lower, with some literally going for broke (see The 1p Club). However, for The Banker this is his precious baby and he fiercely guards it round the clock.

Big Winners These are the people who have done the most to disprove the myth of invincibility that The Banker likes to surround himself with, for they have won £50,000 and over.

Blues Cruise They do say that taking a cruise is good for one's wellbeing, and in Deal or No Deal, a Blues Cruise can make a player very happy indeed. It involves opening a bunch of blue numbers in succession, thereby getting rid of a lot of low amounts and leaving the player with an improved chance of a high win.

Break A chance for the viewer to enjoy some advertisements (or indeed make a nice cup of tea). In the lead-up to every ad break, Noel tries to offer a 'witty' way to introduce it, perhaps suggesting to the player that they 'break a leg'.

Board This is the large, illuminated sign that shows all the amounts of money that are on offer. It marks a player's progress as they knock different amounts off the board. The Banker, who likes to think of himself as Chairman of this Board, always claims that what's left up can transfix a player – and then reminds them that they might perhaps wish to cut their potential losses and accept his more-than-fair offer.

Boxes, The (see 22 above).

Crazy Chair, The Noel's name for the stool the contestants are offered at the beginning of a game. Some players use it as a vague base from which they prowl around the set. Noel named it the Crazy Chair because, like the driver's seat in a car, once certain people are in it, they go a little mad and are no longer the person they seemed to be.

Damage limitation territory A phrase used by Noel when a player has lost most of the big numbers, and is now trying to hit some blues to improve their chances of landing a good offer from The Banker.

Dream Factory The Endemol West shed, oops, studio, where dreams are made and dashed. The production hub for the show.

East Wing, The Or the right hand side of the set where 11 players stand behind their boxes. [See also West Wing] Between filming, it has been known for banter to be fierce between the two wings as each show their true competitive nature.

Hokey Cokey, The The official dance of Deal or No Deal. Not content with having put their right hands in and out of blue and red boxes all day, it has become a Deal or No Deal tradition that every night at 10.30 contestants put their left legs in, take their left legs out and shake them all about, in their hotel lobby. [See Hotel, below].

Hotel The luxurious hostelry situated in the lush, rolling greensward of England where contestants get to stay together for as many weeks as filming takes. The lucky so-and-sos even get to bring family and friends to stay with them if they want. It is here that such great team spirit is forged that, as one contestant put it, it feels as if you're at a family wedding. (Alcohol and the hokey cokey, see above, may also help in this respect.) Indeed, it is sometimes said that no one ever wants to leave.

Independent Adjudicator, The The only person who knows where the money is.

Lucky Hat, The An especially floppy straw-like bonnet that Noel puts on when he feels a player is in need of a little luck. Combined with the Lucky Teabag (see below), the results can be spectacular.

Lucky Teabag, The A teabag that is kept in the studio kitchen and revered as a relic because of its legendary luck-bringing properties. When Lance in series two had a sniff of the teabag before his game, he subsequently went on to win £87,000 from The Banker. That's some teabag.

Mug, The Because nothing beats a nice mug of tea in the afternoon, contestants get a huge mug with a question mark on the front, and something else on the bottom, when they fancy a cuppa. As the show can go on for two hours, remember, they need some sustenance.

Newbies Every day three new contestants are introduced into the remaining members of the original 22 after the three players go out. These are the 'newbies' and everyone's really nice to them, as you'd expect.

Noel's Catchphrases

The whole world loves a catchphrase and Noel is positively smitten with his. And there are so many! They're encouraging, friendly, warm and as corny as a chicken's breakfast, but he loves them. And so do we. Here are a few of the best:

'(Name), Welcome to the game!'

'Deal or No Deal?'

'Don't be seduced by the board!'

'Risk, reward and timing.'

'Keep it low, keep it blue.'

'NOT the quarter of a million, NOT the hundred thousand!'

'The right deal, at the right time!'

'It's now all or peanuts.'

'This is the best game we have ever had.'

'It's your show.'

'I think you'll be back.'

'No! No! No!'

'Play the money, don't play the game.'

'We don't want to see one of the big numbers!'

'This could potentially be the highest offer we have ever had!'

'Let's keep it blue, (name),' just before a box is opened.

'I'm calling a break.'

Noel's Book At the beginning of the show contestants are often asked if they want to write down the sum they hope to take away with them in Noel's book. Sometimes this is shown to the banker, which of course can increase tension – he might offer them something just over their sum, for instance, to tempt them away from what might be a much bigger sum still on the board. Who said everything in life was fair?

Pound Table, The The table at which the player perches or stands as they play the game, and to which Noel comes, goes and leans. So far no one has seen fit to actually pound on the table, but it can only be a matter of time...

Power Five, The The top five sums of money that can be won by a player—in ascending order, they are £35,000, £50,000, £75,000, £100,000 and £250,000.

Rapid Round, A Also known as 'a quickie'. In the first round of any game a player has to open five boxes before The Banker will make an offer. Subsequently, rapid rounds, where three boxes are opened at a time, can be played. At such times The Banker holds his breath, as if underwater.

Red Box Club, The A not-so-secret society formed by ex-players and fans who are passionate about Deal or No Deal. They have their own websites, hold reunions, and generally converse online about what a great time they had and continue to have watching new players give The Banker a thrashing.

Red Mist Not a perfume launched by The Banker (although, now someone's mentioned it...), but the terrible fog that descends upon a player, obscuring all else available to them on the board except that one high red number. Under the influence of the Red Mist they go for it, risking all and often losing it, too.

Red Run A Deal or No Deal equivalent of the Spanish bull run, where the player is left feeling gored and dazed by a high number of reds revealed in sequence. Poor Nick Bain got 8 in a row, and ended up founding the 1p

Club (see above).

Risk Tolerance The assessment made by The Banker on what any player will take if offered, in relation to what they might get. He'll always claim to know more about a player's risk tolerance – or exactly how far they'll go before crashing and burning and giving in to him – than the players themselves. There are a few that have surprised him. But not many.

Safety Net What Noel usually calls a good number of reds still on the board as the game progresses. A decent number of reds in middle rounds increases the chances that the player will knock out the blues before they're gone.

Swap, The The Banker can offer to swap one numbered box for another – usually but not always at the end of the game, or perhaps earlier if the player has unwisely professed a preference for a number. The Swap is a perfect example of how The Banker's twisted brain works when he wants to turn the screws on some poor player. They have to decide whether to swap or not...

Theatre Of Dreams, The What some non-Manchester United fans call the Endemol West studios (see Dream Factory, above). In fact only Old Trafford can be called the Theatre of Dreams, and they've probably trademarked the phrase.

Walk of Wealth, The That 'ready for my close-up Mr DeMille' moment when, after the 22 players have filed in and are standing behind their boxes, the spotlight focuses on The One. The player who is chosen then walks the Walk of Wealth down to the Crazy Chair as the applause envelopes them, the lights reflect from their shining eyes and they know that it's their show, their time, their moment...!

West Wing, The Nothing to do either with George Bush's White House (nor 'President' Martin Sheen's either), it's the line-up of the 11 contestants who stand on the left-hand side of the studio, opposite the East Wing (see above).